Dictionary of Art

BROCKHAMPTON PRESS
LONDON

A

Aalto, Alvar (1898-1976) Finnish architect who influenced 20th-century architecture away from the strong geometric shapes of CONSTRUCTIVISM towards softer curves and more irregular forms, also a designer of Artek furniture. In Finland he worked on postwar reconstruction in civic and industrial design. Major exhibitions were in Paris (1937) and New York (1938). He taught architecture at the Massachusetts Institute of Technology (1948-1950). Important works include the War Memorial at Suomussalmi (1960) and the town hall at Saynatsalo (1950-2).

Abbey, Edwin Austen (1852-1911) American illustrator and painter of historical scenes. He worked both in the US and England and was the official painter at the coronation of Edward VII in 1902. He illustrated popular magazines, such as *Harper's,* and one of his best-known paintings is the portrait of *Richard, Duke of Gloucester, and Lady Anne.*

abstract art Art that intentionally avoids representation of the observed world. Abstraction has long been a feature of the decorative arts and to a large degree continues to dominate the art of the 20th-century. There are two distinct trends: one towards an ordered, hard-edged CONSTRUCTIVISM, as in the works of MONDRIAN; the other leaning to a freer, more expressionistic reduction of forms, as e.g. in the CUBISM painting of CÉZANNE.

abstract expressionism Art that is based on freedom of expression, spontaneity and random composition and is characterized by loose, unrestrained brushwork and often indistinct forms, usually on large canvases. The works may or may not be figurative. The term mainly applies to an art movement of the 1940s in New York, although it was first used in 1919 with reference to the early abstract work of KANDINSKY. Inspired by SURREALISM, the movement represented a breakaway from the realism hitherto dominant in American art and went on to influence European art in the 1950s. Artists associated with the movement include DE KOONING, POLLOCK, KLINE and GORKY, as well as the COLOUR FIELD painters, ROTHKO and NEWMAN.

academy of art An institution of professional artists or scholars. The word derives from Greek and refers to a place of learning, but it was specifically the name of the grove where Plato taught his students. The first academy of art was the Accademia del Disegno, founded in Florence in 1563; MICHELANGELO was one of its first directors. Its purpose was to raise the artist's status from that of an artisan by teaching art theory as well as practical skills. Academies drew their authority and financial support from the church, royalty or rich families, like the

MEDICI, and the proliferation of academies across Europe in the 18th century was largely under state control, the Royal Academy in the UK, founded in 1768, being an exception. The National Academy of Design was founded in the US in 1924 by a breakaway group of young members from the American Academy of Fine Arts, founded in 1802.

acrylic paint A versatile synthetic paint that is quick-drying and can be used in thick, heavy layers or thin washes on almost any surface. A range of matt or gloss finishes can be achieved by the use of additives.

action painting A form of ABSTRACT EXPRESSIONISM in which the paint is applied to the canvas in the course of a series of actions or movements by the artist. This may involve dancing, cycling or rolling about on the canvas to spread and mix the wet paint. In a less random technique the artist might paint the silhouette of a model in various poses against the canvas. Jackson POLLOCK was a prominent exponent of action painting.

Adam, Robert (1728-92) Scottish architect famous for his individualistic interpretations of Palladian and REN-AISSANCE styles in domestic architecture. He designed numerous town houses in London, e.g. 20 Portman Square (1777), formerly the Courtauld Institute of Art, and Chandos House (1771); and he transformed old houses, such as those at Syon (1726-9) and at Osterley (1761-80), both near London. He also worked on the lay-out of Charlotte Square (1791) and Register House

(1774-92) in Edinburgh. His designs usually included interior decor and furnishings down to the smallest details, and his style has been widely imitated. His brother, **James Adam** (1730-94), worked with him as a draughtsman and also designed buildings of his own.

Adams, Ansel (1902-84) American photographer. Born in San Francisco, he trained as a pianist before becoming a photographer in 1930. The clarity and detail of his landscapes, mainly of the southwest US of the 1930s, represented a move away from the painterly trends in mainstream art and photography. He helped to initiate the first photography departments in museums and colleges and wrote a number of technical handbooks on the subject.

Adams, Charles Samuel (1912-) American cartoonist. Born in New Jersey, he worked for *New Yorker* magazine from 1935 and became particularly well known for his humorously macabre style.

Aeken, Jerom van *see* **Bosch, Hieronymus**

aestheticism The side of the debate that argues that the value of a work of art is in its inherent beauty and not in any moral, religious or political message it might carry. Indeed, in the late 18th century, at the height of the debate, it was suggested that any such message actually detracted from the value of the work. The famous court case between Ruskin and Whistler arose out of aesthetic controversy, although of a slightly different nature. Since the beginning of the 20th century a more tolerant attitude has generally prevailed.

aesthetics An area of philosophy concerning the ideals of taste and beauty and providing criteria for critical study of the arts. The term was coined in the mid-18th century by the German philosopher Alexander Baumgarten, and in the 20th century came to include a wider theory of natural beauty.

African art A term generally used to describe African tribal art in the countries south of the Sahara Desert. Much of this art is of a group nature, in that it has cultural and religious significance at its heart rather than individual ambition. Examples of typical art forms include richly carved wooden masks and figures. Body art is also important in tribal ritual and may involve scarring, tattooing or disfigurement of parts of the body, although it can also make use of paint, beads and feathers. Brightly coloured batiks and printed fabrics are a more recent feature of this rich heritage. African tribal art had a marked influence on 20th-century art styles, as in the works of PICASSO and CÉZANNE.

air brush An atomizer, powered by compressed air, that is used to spray paint. It is shaped like a large fountain pen and produces a fine mist of colour, giving delicate tonal gradations and a smooth finish. Its principal use is in the fields of advertising and graphic design.

alabaster A fine-grained type of gypsum that can be translucent, white or streaked with colour. It is soft and easy to carve and is therefore a popular medium for decorative artefacts and statues. It is not as strong or weather-resistant as marble, and is not often used for outdoor works.

Albers, Josef (1888-1976) German-born American painter and designer. He taught at the BAUHAUS until its closure in 1933, when he emigrated to the US, becoming an American citizen in 1939. His early work concentrated on stained glass, the design of utility objects and furniture. He took his Bauhaus ideas to the Black Mountain College in North Carolina and to Harvard University before moving to Yale University in 1950. He outlined his theories on colour relationships in *The Intersection of Color* (1963). His series of paintings entitled *Homage to the Square* explore these relationships through various compositions of flat squares set one inside the other.

Albert, Calvin (1918-) American sculptor in the school of ABSTRACT EXPRESSIONISM. Much of his work involved special metal welding techniques, and he undertook commissions for decorative sculptures in churches and synagogues. His one-man shows were in Chicago (1941) and New York (1944); a retrospective exhibition was shown at the Jewish Museum (1960) and he also participated in group exhibitions.

Alberti, Leon Battista (1404-72) Italian writer, architect, sculptor and painter. Born in Genoa, he worked mainly in Rome and Florence. His most famous written works are on art theory, including *On Painting* (*De Pictura*, 1435), *On Sculpture* (*De Statua*, *c*.1440) and his life's work, *On Architecture* (*De Re Aedificatoria,* 1485), the first treatise on architecture ever to be printed. His architectural designs include the facade of the Church of San Francesco in Rimini and that of Santa Maria Novella in Florence, but little of his painting or sculpture has survived. A prominent RENAISSANCE figure, his wide-ranging interests and talents, including music and athletics, are representative of the "universal man" ideal of his humanist views.

Algardi, Alessandro (*c.*1595-1654) Italian BAROQUE sculptor. Born in Bologna, he worked in Rome from 1625 and was patronized by Pope Innocent X, mainly because his style of work was given less to contortion and violent action than his contemporary BERNINI. His major works include the tomb of Leo Xl (*c.*1645) in Rome and the sculptured group, *The Decapitation of Saint Paul,* in Bologna.

Allston, Washington (1779-1843) American landscape painter and leading figure in the beginnings of ROMANTICISM in the US. He worked mainly in Boston, apart from two lengthy periods in England, during the first of which (1801-8) he studied at the Royal Academy under Benjamin WEST. His work was large in scale and concentrated on the monumental, mysterious and dramatic elements of nature and religious subjects. Notable examples include *The Rising of a Thunderstorm at Sea* and *Dead Man Revived.* His later works were poetic and dreamlike in character, as in *Moonlit Landscape.* Samuel

MORSE was his pupil. *See also* HUDSON RIVER SCHOOL.

Alma-Tadema, Sir Lawrence (1836-1912) Dutch-born painter who moved to England in 1870, where he enjoyed a highly successful career. He painted historical scenes, in particular of classical Greece and Rome, and designed stage sets for the Roman plays of Shakespeare. His paintings often included beautiful women, usually in a sentimental style but occasionally displaying eroticism, as in *In the Tepidarium* (1881). Most of his works contain an opus number in roman numerals.

Altamira The site in northern Spain of prehistoric rock paintings dating from about 13000BC, in 1879 the first ever to be discovered. Originally dismissed as forgeries, their age and authenticity were accepted as genuine only in the early 20th century. A variety of animals painted in a lively, naturalistic manner are depicted, including bison, aurochs and wild horses.

altarpiece A decorated wall, screen or sectional painting set behind the altar of a Christian church, a feature of church decor dating from the 11th century. There are two forms: a retable can be fairly large and complex, rising from floor level; a reredos is often smaller and may stand on the altar itself or on a pedestal behind it.

Altdorfer, Albrecht (1480-1538) German painter and printmaker. A major figure of the so-called Danube School of painters who developed the importance of landscape, his work is characterized by a fantastic inventiveness, distortion of figures and brilliant effects of colour and light. His themes were mainly religious, but his outstanding contribution to art is in the development of landscape painting as a genre in its own right. Notable among his paintings are *St George and the Dragon* (1510), *Susannah and the Elders* (1526) and *The Battle of Alexander and Darius on the Issus* (1529), which was a commission from Duke William lV of Bavaria.

Ammanati, Bartolomeo (1511-92) Italian sculptor and architect. He worked in Venice and Rome as well as in Florence, where he won a commission to create the famous fountain depicting a huge marble statue of *Neptune* with bronze nymphs. His architectural works include the Ponte Santa Trinità and the court of the Pitti Palace, both in Florence. In later life he destroyed many of his nude statues and recanted his secular works under the influence of counter-Reformation piety.

Ancients,The A group of ROMANTIC artists working in England between 1824 and the early 1830s. PALMER was a leading member of the group, which also included RICHMOND and CALVERT. Their work was mainly pastoral in theme, much inspired by BLAKE's illustrations of Virgil.

Andre, Carl (1935-   ) American sculptor whose Minimalist style emphasizes the real in art as opposed to the metaphoric. His systematic arrangements of single objects in horizontal pattern are intended to focus attention on the relationships between the objects and their surroundings. Famous among his works are his *144*

Pieces of Lead and *Equivalent VIII*, the "Tate bricks" that so outraged the British art public in 1976.

Andrea del Castagno (*c*.1421-57) Florentine artist. One of the leading painters of his generation, his potentially outstanding career was cut short by his death from plague. His earliest surviving works are the frescos in San Terassio presso San Zaccaria in Venice, but his best-known works are in Florence, in particular the *Passion of Christ* (1445-50) in the convent of Santa Apollonia, which is now in the Castagno Museum. The monumental realism of his style is comparable with the work of DONATELLO, as in, for example, *The Vision of St Jerome* at SS Annunziata in Florence.

Andrea del Sarto (1486-1530) Florentine painter, a pupil of PIERO DI COSIMO and a contemporary of Fra BARTOLOMMEO who, along with RAPHAEL, influenced his elegant, classical style. His best-known works are his fresco cycles in the cloisters of SS Annunziata and his Uffizi altarpiece, *The Madonna of the Harpies*. A major figure of the high RENAISSANCE, his work was among the greatest examples of contemporary classical art.

Angelico, Fra [Guido di Pietro] (*c*.1400-1455) Dominican monk and Florentine painter of the early RENAISSANCE. All his work is religious in character, one of the earliest and most famous being *The Annunciation* 1428). At the same time, his contribution to the understanding of perspective and the development of complex landscape settings is undeniably progressive and professional, as in *Descent from the Cross* (1440). His major work is the series of about fifty frescos (most of them in the cells) in his monastery of San Marco, now a museum housing a large collection of his art.

Anglo-Saxon art A term for works of art produced in England between AD 5 and 1066. The major source of surviving artefacts is the 7th-century excavation site at Sutton Hoo, and much of the Anglo-Saxon jewellery collection at the British Museum comes from there. The abstract plant and animal designs show the influences of Celtic art typical of Anglo-Saxon craft. The late 7th and early 8th centuries saw the production of the Lindisfarne Gospels in the kingdom of Northumbria. These are famous for their delicate interwoven designs, reminiscent of Irish illuminations, as in the Book of Kells. The other centre for manuscript production was the Winchester school of the 10th century.

Antique, The Remains of ancient art, in particular Greek and Roman statues, which were taken as a standard of classical order and beauty in the representation of the human form by RENAISSANCE and NEO-CLASSICAL artists.

Antonello da Messina (*c*. 1430-79) Sicilian painter, whose work helped to popularize oil painting in Italy. His work displays a strong Flemish influence in its light, atmosphere and attention to detail, as in some of his bust-length portraits. The composition and modelling of his figures, however, owe much to Italian sculpture. A good example of this combination is his *Crucifixion* in London's National Gallery.

Apelles Greek painter from the 4th century BC and court painter to Philip of Macedon and Alexander the Great. None of his work has survived and his fame is due to the enthusiasm of classical authors, whose detailed descriptions of his work later inspired RENAISSANCE artists such as BOTTICELLI and TITIAN.

Apollinaire, Guillaume (1880-1918) French art critic and writer of great influence among avant-garde artists and poets at the beginning of the 20th century. A friend of PICASSO and a champion of CUBISM, he published *The Cubist Painters* in 1913. He was also a supporter of ORPHISM and FUTURISM. He originated the term SURREALISM in 1917 in a preface to his play *The Breasts of Tiresias*. He was wounded in World War I and subsequently died of Spanish influenza.

Apollodorus Athenian painter from the 5th century BC called Sciagraphus because, according to Pliny, he was the first artist to depict light and shadow in the modelling of his figures, an important development in art history.

applied arts Art that serves a useful purpose or that ornaments functional objects; often a synonym for design. Subjects included under this term are architecture, interior design, ceramics, furniture, graphics, etc. These are usually contrasted with the **fine arts** of painting, drawing, sculpture printmaking, etc, and the division became more distinct at the time of the Industrial Revolution and

the emergence of AESTHETICISM. This division is still a
matter of important debate.

aquarelle The French term for watercolour painting,
where a water-based paint is applied to dampened paper
in thin glazes that are gradually built up into areas of
varying tone.

aquatint An etching technique where a resin-coated
metal plate is placed in a bath of acid that bites into the
resin, producing a pitted surface. The depth of tone in-
tensifies the longer the plate remains in the acid, and areas required to be lighter in tone are "stopped out," using
washes of varnish. The finished print resembles a watercolour wash, and the technique of overlaying separate
plates of different colours can be used to build up a range
of depth and colour. The process is often combined with
linear etching.

Archipenko, Alexander (1887-1946) Ukrainian-born
American sculptor who studied briefly at Kiev and exhibited in group shows in Moscow before moving to
Paris. From 1910 he had links with CUBISM and was a
member of the SECTION D'OR group. He opened his own
school in 1912. The geometric style of his early work explored extreme simplifications of form and the importance of enclosed voids in sculpture. Experiments with a
variety of media and with colour evolved into a polychrome relief style he called "sculpto-peinture." He became an American citizen in 1928 and taught in a
number of establishments, including the New Bauhaus

and his own schools in Chicago and New York. Later experiments in movement and light resulted in perspex sculptures lit from within. His influence on 20th-century European and American sculpture has been considerable.

Armory Show The international exhibition of modern art held at the 69th Regimental Armory in New York in 1913, one of the most influential exhibitions ever shown in the US. Organized by an association of painters and sculptors, including HENRI and DAVIES, it was effectively two exhibitions in one. It represented not only a fine cross-section of contemporary American art but also a massive selection of modern European art, a total of around 1,600 works. It toured the US, arousing great controversy and excitement among the 250,000 people who paid to see it, but it served the function of restoring the life and vitality of contemporary art and critical debate in the US.

Arnolfo di Cambio (1245-1302?) Italian sculptor and architect,who studied in Pisa under Nicola PISANO before moving to Rome in 1277, where he worked principally on Papal tombs. The best surviving example is that of Cardinal de Braye (*d.*1293) in San Dominico, which influenced the style of wall tombs for the next hundred years. He designed the altar canopies for San Paulo fuori le Mura (1285) and Santa Cecilia in Trastevere (1293), and was one of the architects of Florence Cathedral. The bronze statue of *St Peter* in Rome is also attributed to

him, and he was one of the most important Italian architects in the Gothic style.

Arp, Jean *or* **Hans** (1887-1966) French abstract sculptor
of great merit. He had early links with the BLAUE REITER
movement and later with CUBISM and SURREALISM. Arp
worked on the development of collage together with the
Swiss painter, **Sophie Taeuber** (1889-1943), who later
became his wife, and was a founder of the Dada group.
His later work involved polychrome relief sculpture and
a style he called "creative abstraction," concerned with
organic forms while not actually representing plant or
animal life.

Art Autre or **Art Informel** A name coined by art critic
Michel Tapie in *Un Art Autre* (1952); he used it to describe non-geometric ABSTRACT EXPRESSIONISM.

Art Brut The work of anyone not linked to the art world
either as professional or amateur, for example psychiat-
ric patients or prisoners, etc. The term can also include
graffiti and the work of young children. It refers to any
work uninfluenced by the art world and its fashions. *See
also* DUBUFFET.

Art Deco The decorative art of the 1920s and 30s in Europe and North America, originally called Jazz Modern.
It was classical in style, with slender, symmetrical, geometric or rectilinear forms. Major influences were ART
NOUVEAU architecture and ideas from the ARTS AND
CRAFTS movement and the BAUHAUS. The simplicity of
style was easily adaptable to modern industrial produc-

tion methods and contemporary materials, especially plastics. This resulted in a proliferation of utility items, jewellery and furniture in an elegant streamlined form, as well as simplification and streamlining of interior decor and architecture.

Art Nouveau A style of decorative art influential and popular between 1890 and World War I in Europe and North America. Art Nouveau was primarily a design style with its main effects being seen in applied art, graphics, furniture and fabric design and in architecture. In the fine arts it represented a move away from historical realism, but was not as vigorous or dominant as IMPRESSIONISM or CUBISM. Art Nouveau design is characterized by flowing organic forms and asymmetric linear structures, although architectural and calligraphic forms were more austere and reserved. Its principal exponents were the Scottish architect and designer **Charles Rennie Mackintosh** (1868-1928) and the American designer **Louis Comfort Tiffany** (1848-1933). Art Nouveau has enjoyed a revival of popularity in the 1970s and 80s.

Arts and Crafts Movement An English movement in the decorative arts towards the end of the 19th century. It was based on the ideas of the art critic John RUSKIN and the architect A.W. Pugin, with reference to the medieval guilds system, and took its name from the Arts and Crafts Exhibition Society formed in 1888. The motive was to re-establish the value of handcrafted objects at a time of increasing mass-production and industrialization. Designers in the movement, with a variety of styles, attempted to produce functional objects of an aesthetically pleasing nature. The most active and important leader of the movement was William MORRIS.

Arundel, Thomas Howard, 2nd Earl of (1586-1646) English patron of the arts, collector and antiquarian, and also a prominent figure at the court of Charles I. In 1613 he went to Italy to carry out archaeological work in Rome with the architect Inigo Jones. He was a patron of RUBENS and van DYCK, each of whom painted his portrait. His impressive art collection was broken up after his death, although the bulk of his classical sculpture is in the Ashmolean Museum in Oxford.

ascription *see* **attribution**.

Ashcan School A group of American painters of urban realism between 1908 and 1918. Its leading members were HENRI, LUKS, GLACKENS, and SHINN, although others were associated with them, including HOPPER, BELLOWS and MAURER. Their joint aim was to declare themselves primarily American painters, and they painted what they saw as American life, generally rejecting subject matter of academic approval. Among their influences were the works of DAUMIER and GOYA.

assemblage Any sculptural type of construction using found objects, from pieces of painted wood to old shoes. *See also* COLLAGE.

atelier The French term for an artist's studio. In 19th-century France, an *atelier libre* was a studio where artists could go to paint a model. No formal tuition was provided, and a small fee was charged. DELACROIX, COURBET and several of the Impressionists, e.g. PISSARRO and CÉZANNE, used the Atelier Julian, which was opened in 1860 and was later used by MATISSE, LÉGER and most of the NABIS.

attribution *or* **ascription** The assigning of an unsigned picture to a painter, using similarity of style or subject as the basis.

Audubon, John James (1784-1851) American naturalist and artist. Born in the West Indies and brought up in France, he studied drawing with DAVID before moving to America in 1803. He continued to draw and paint while working as a taxidermist, and his passion for ornithology resulted in the magnificent plates for his famous *Birds of America.* This was published by the London firm of Havell and Son between 1827 and 1838. A subsequent series, *The Viviparous Quadrupeds of North America*, was completed by his sons after his death. His drawings are lively and colourful and combine excellent draughtsmanship with scientific accuracy. *Birds of America* is among the most valuable and beautiful of illustrated books.

Auerbach, Frank (1931-) German-born British painter, he worked in England from 1939 and was influenced by BOMBERG, under whom he trained. Figures and portraits predominate in his work, executed either in chalk and charcoal or a heavy impasto of oil paint.

autograph A term used to denote a painting by one artist only, and not assisted by pupils or assistants.

Automatistes *see* **Borduas, Paul Emile**.

Avery, Milton (1893-1965) American self-taught painter, his early influences were MATISSE and the FAUVISTS. Although he later painted some landscapes in a more EXPRESSIONIST style, his work is mainly characterized by flat areas of thin paint in soft, rounded, flowing shapes, using closely keyed interacting colours. His best-known paintings include *Mother and Child* (1944) and *Swimmers and Sunbathers* (1945).

Ayres, Gillian, (1930-) British painter much influenced in her early work by American ABSTRACT EXPRESSIONISM, particularly the work of Jackson POLLOCK. In the 1960s she moved towards tighter, organic forms, although her later work is again looser and more sensuous, concentrating on intensity of colours.

B

Baburen, Dirck van *see* **Utrecht School**

Bacon, Francis (1909-92) Irish-born British painter, he moved to London in 1925 where he set up as an interior decorator. His early work attracted little attention and he destroyed much of it. He later became famous almost overnight, in April 1945, when he exhibited *Figure in a Landscape* and the now well-known triptych *Three Studies for Figures at the Base of the Crucifixion.* His works depict a horror-fantasy existence, concentrating on the repulsive aspects of human shape in weird landscapes or spaces, twisted and contorted in his handling of the paint, He also executed a series of paintings based on the portrait, by VELAZQUEZ, of Pope Innocent X. Bacon is an important but isolated figure in British art.

Bakst, Léon (1866-1924) Russian designer and painter. He trained at the Academy of Art in Moscow and, after a period in Paris, moved to St Petersburg in 1900. He established himself as a portraitist and illustrator and designed spectacular ballet sets for the theatres, including the Russian Ballet. He also had his own school where Marc CHAGALL and the dancer Nijinsky were among his pupils. He was a close friend and associate of Diaghilev, and a member of the *Mir Iskusstra* group.

Baldung Grien, Hans (1484-1545) German engraver and painter thought to have worked in DÜRER's workshop and certainly influenced by him, as in *The Knight, Death and the Maiden* (1505). Later influences include GRÜNEWALD, and this can be seen in the use of colour and distortion in his major work, the altarpiece for the cathedral at Freiburg (1512-17). His teutonic taste for the gruesome and macabre is evident in the themes of his woodcuts, notably *The Bewitched Stable Boy* (1544).

Barbizon School A group of French landscape painters in the 1840s who based their art on direct study from nature. Their initial influences included CONSTABLE and BONINGTON as well as some of the Dutch landscape painters. Their advanced ideas represented a move away from academic conventions, and their interest in daylight effects and their bold use of colour helped prepare the way for IMPRESSIONISM. Leading members of the group included DAUBIGNY and Théodore ROUSSEAU.

Barlach, Ernst (1870-1938) German EXPRESSIONIST sculptor, who studied in Hamburg, Dresden and Paris and worked in Berlin until 1901. In 1906 he travelled in Russia and there was impressed by peasant building expressiveness. This led him to a simplified, block-like style of carving, intense in its emotional range and imbued with the atmosphere of the medieval gothic carvings that formed a vital part of his sculptural inspiration. Notable among his works is the war memorial at Gustrow Cathedral. His former studio at Gustrow and the Barlachhaus in Hamburg both contain collections of his work.

Barnard, George Grey (1863-1938) American sculptor. He studied in Chicago and Paris and was inspired by a line from Victor Hugo to produce his best-known work, *The Nature of Man,* which he exhibited in the Paris Salon in 1894. Other works in New York include *The God Pan,* in Central Park, and *Two Natures,* in the Metropolitan Museum.

Baroque A cultural movement in art, music and science in the 17th century. In terms of art history, the area of reference is slightly broader and takes in the late 16th and early 18th centuries. It specifically indicates the stage between the MANNERISM of the late High RENAISSANCE and ROCOCO, into which Baroque developed. As a style it is characterized by movement, rhetoric and emotion, stemming from the achievements of the High Renaissance, and it represented a reaction away from Mannerist attitudes and techniques. CARAVAGGIO was among its leading figures when it first began in Rome; BERNINI took prominence in High Baroque as the movement developed in the 1620s. RUBENS' series on the *Life of Maria de' Medici* marks a peak in Baroque painting, and REMBRANDT'S work reflected Baroque trends for part of his career, Adjectivally, "baroque" can also be used to describe art from any age that displays the richness and dynamism associated with the movement.

Barry, James (1741-1806) Irish painter patronized and financed in his early career by the writer Edmund Burke. He was a history painter in the Grand Manner and professor of painting at the Royal Academy in London from 1782. His most famous and ambitious work is *The Progress of Human Culture* (1777-83), which he painted gratis for the Society of Arts. His uncompromising egotism caused his expulsion from the Academy in 1799.

Bartholdi, Frédéric Auguste (1834-1904) French sculptor, famous for his monumental sculptures, the most notable of which is *Liberty Enlightening the World*, the "Statue of Liberty" in New York Bay.

Bartolommeo, Fra [Baccio della Porta] (*c.*1472-1571) Florentine painter of the High RENAISSANCE and, from 1880, a monk in San Marco, the convent where Fra ANGELICO had worked. Bartolommeo was an excellent draughtsman, and his prolific, lively drawings communicate emotions more easily than his rather austere painting style with its solid, classical figures. He was a contemporary of RAPHAEL and had a notable influence on ANDREA DEL SARTO. Famous among his works are *The Vision of St Bernard, The Marriage of St Catherine* and the *Salvador Mundi*.

Baskin, Leonard (1929-) American sculptor, graphic arts teacher and founder of the Gehenna press. A self-styled "moral realist," his work has affinities with EX-PRESSIONISM and is concerned with the isolation and vulnerability of the human figure. A retrospective show of his work was held in 1962 at Bowdoin College Museum of Art.

Bassano, Jacopo da Ponte.(*c.*1510-92) Italian painter, a prominent member of a family of painters from the town of Bassano. Jacopo trained with his father, **Francesco the elder** (*c.* 1475-1539) and was briefly a pupil of VERONESE in Venice. Jacopo's early work is of Biblical scenes in a pastoral style, in which his vividly painted figures and animals are full of life. His style later became more refined during a vogue for prints after RAPHAEL and PARMIGIANINO, and he used chiaroscuro effects in his more mature compositions. His four sons were all artists, the most important being **Francesco** (1549-92), who continued the Biblical and pastoral themes of his father as well as being a painter of historical scenes, and **Leandro** (1557-1622), who also followed the rustic genre, but specialized in painting altarpieces. Both were important artists in the MANNERIST tradition.

Bauhaus German school of architecture and applied arts founded by the architect **Walter Gropius** (1883-1969) at Weimar in 1919. One of its aims, in common with the ARTS AND CRAFTS MOVEMENT in England, was to narrow the gap between fine and applied arts; the other was to focus on architecture as the environment of art. Each student took a six-month foundation course in practical craft skills such as weaving, glass painting and metalwork. Among the first masters at Weimar were the EX-

PRESSIONIST painters KLEE and KANDINSKY. A more CONSTRUCTIVIST influence came with ALBERS and MOHOLY-NAGY, when the Bauhaus moved to Dessau in 1925. Later came a shift in emphasis from craftsmanship towards industrialized mass-production. Gropius resigned from the Bauhaus in 1928; it was moved to Berlin in 1932 and was closed by the Nazis in 1933. A number of Bauhaus masters emigrated to the US, where their ideas continued to be influential.

Bearden, Romare (1914-) American painter from Charlotte, North Carolina. His work is concerned with the life experience of black Americans. His COLLAGES and acrylic paintings are characterized by vibrant energy and expressiveness. One of his most successful works is *The Dove* (1946), and exhibitions include a retrospective in 1968 at the State University of New York and a one-man show in 1970 at the Museum of Modern Art in New York.

Beardsley, Aubrey Vincent (1872-98) English illustrator in the ART NOUVEAU style and a prominent figure of AESTHETICISM in the 1890s. Although he died at the early age of 25, he was a prolific artist. His distinctive use of black and white line and pattern and his penchant for the morbid and grotesque made him one of the most controversial illustrators of his time. His first set of illustrations was for the *Mort d'Arthur* published by Dent, and he rose to fame with his work for Oscar Wilde's *Salomé* and the periodical *The Yellow Book*. Other notable works include drawings for *The Rape of The Lock,* by Alexander Pope, and the magazine *Savoy.*

Beckmann, Max (1884-1950) German painter who studied at Weimar and also in Paris and Italy before moving to Berlin in 1904. Originally an IMPRESSIONIST and a member of the SEZESSION, his own experiences, and the misery and despair he witnessed during World War I led him to a more distorted, EXPRESSIONISTIC style reminiscent of German Gothic art, as in *The Night* (1919). His expressionism is not abstract but lies closer to social realism in its commitment to moral statements on human suffering and responsiveness. From 1932 he painted a series of nine triptychs outlining these themes, the best known being *Departure* (1932). He was one of the most important German expressionist painters.

Bell, Vanessa (1879-1961) British painter and leading figure of the Bloomsbury group. Her early work is in a POST-IMPRESSIONIST style, but became more formal and design-orientated with her painting *Studland Beach* (1912). After a period of total abstraction, her later work returned to a more traditional form.

Bellany, John (1942-) Scottish painter who studied at Edinburgh College of Art and was a prominent figure in the renaissance movement in Scottish art in the 1960s. His work usually centres on the human figure, and human values are of prime importance. His early works, based on the working lives of fishermen, are full of dignity, portraying the heroic and the tragic in everyday hu-

man existence. His heritage is in the North European tradition and the influence of Max BECKMANN, "social real-
ist" EXPRESSIONISM. This is apparent in the triptych *Alle-gory* and in Bellany's development of a symbolic "language" in his paintings.

Bellini, Giovanni (1430-1516) Venetian painter and an
important member of a family of artists. His early Gothic
style derives from the teaching of his father **Jacopo**
(*c.*1400-1470) but his later work involves a much more
subtle use of tone and colour. He was influenced by his
brother-in-law, MANTEGNA, and, in the use of oil paint, by
ANTONELLO DA MESSINA, who visited Venice in 1475-76.
His vision is of a classical, contemplative dignity, and an
important feature of his work is the total integration of
figures in a landscape that enhances the atmosphere. A
common theme is the Madonna and Child, of which the
Barberini Madonna is a notable example. GIORGIONE and
TITIAN were among his pupils. His brother **Gentile**
(*c.*1430-1507) was official painter to the Doge of Venice
from 1474 and is known to have painted murals and portraits for Sultan Mehmet II while he was court envoy at
Istanbul. Notable among his surviving works are *A Pro-cession of Relics in the Piazza San Marco* (1496) and
The Miracle of Ponte da Lorenzo (1500). Both artists
were indebted to their father for the legacy of his two
sketchbooks containing over 200 drawings that provided
an invaluable source of inspiration for their compositions. The paintings by Mantegna and Giovanni of *The*

Agony in the Garden are taken from Jacopo's drawings.

Bellows, George Wesley (1882-1925) American painter who was a pupil of HENRI and an important influence on the ASHCAN SCHOOL. His painting is characterized by a bold, direct style, and the vigorous realism of his work is evident in *Stag at Sharkey's* (1909), one of a series of paintings of boxers. He was a progressive and outgoing artist and one of the organizers of the ARMORY SHOW.

Benton, Thomas Hart (1889-1975) American painter. He studied in Chicago and Paris and was for a time an abstract CONSTRUCTIVIST painter in the company of MACDONALD-WRIGHT. From the mid-1920s he became a champion of regionalist scene painting and developed his own dramatic style of social realism. Famous among his works are his mural commissions on *American Life* and a series of paintings, *Art of the West.* Jackson POLLOCK was his pupil.

Bernini, Giovanni Lorenzo (1598-1680) Italian BA-ROQUE sculptor, also painter, architect, designer and play-wright. A precocious student, he trained with his father **Pietro** (1562-1629) and was patronized by Cardinal Scipione Borghese. His work demonstrates a tremen-dous insight, energy and virtuosity. Bernini's career and artistic dominance in Rome were established under Pope Urban VIII; he designed the *baldacchino*, or canopy, for St Peter's and built the huge *St Longinus* (1624-38).At this time he was effectively the leading sculptor in Rome. With the accession of Pope Innocent X, Bernini fell from favour to be replaced by ALGARDI. Subsequently his most successful commissions include *The Ecstacy of St Theresa* (1644-52) in Santa Maria della Vittoria and the Piazza and the *Cathedra Petri* in the apse of St Peter's. He was an unrivalled portrait sculptor, whether depicting *Louis XIV of France* or his mistress, *Constanza Buonarelli* (*c*.1635), and his surviving paintings are also of outstanding quality.

Beuys, Joseph (1921-86) German sculptor and important influence on 1970s avante-garde artists. He was a pioneer of "actions" or "happenings," with art as the catalyst that turned human consciousness on its head, as in *Coyote* (1974), in which he spent a week in New York having a conversation with a live coyote. Other performances included the deconstruction and re-assemblage of his own works. A retrospective exhibition of his drawings toured Britain and Ireland in 1974. He was one of the leaders of the *Arte Povera* movement, and there is a collection of his assemblages at Darmstadt Museum.

Bewick, Thomas (1753-1828) British wood-engraver from Newcastle upon Tyne, he became famous for his illustrations of *A General History of Quadrupeds* (1790) and *A History of British Birds* I (1797-1804). He developed the art of wood-engraving into a viable process for clear printed illustrations, and his work is simple with bold tonal contrasts appropriate to the medium.

Biedermeier A style in art and architecture in Austria and Germany between 1815 and 1848. It took its name from a fictional character of the time, Gottlieb Biedermeier, who personified the philistine artistic taste of the middle classes. Architecture associated with the style is solid and utilitarian, paintings are meticulous and devoid of imagination.

Bierstadt, Albert (1830-1902) German-born American landscape painter. From the US, he went to study in Dusseldorf and travelled in Europe, returning to America in 1857. He was a member of the **Rocky Mountain School** of painters who painted landscapes of this formidable countryside, and is famous for his dramatic depiction of it, as in *Thunderstorm on the Rocky Mountains* (1859).

Bingham, George Caleb (1811-79) American painter from Missouri, he was a law and theology student and a cabinet-maker prior to entering the Academy of Fine Arts in 1838. His early work is the most interesting. His precisely composed genre paintings of river life have a fresh and pleasing quality of zest and colour, as in *Fur Traders Descending the Missouri* (1845). His later compositions were influenced by German ROMANTICISM and lost something of their raw charm and individualism. He became professor of art at the University of Missouri in 1877.

Bishop, Isabel (1902-) American painter from Ohio, who studied in New York and taught at the Art Students' League in 1937. She was prominent during the 1930s as a painter of social realism, focussing on the transience of figures in the urban cityscape of Union Square, New York, as in *Waiting* (1938). A one-man exhibition of her work was shown in 1964 at the Brooklyn Museum.

Blake, William (1757-1827) English artist and poet in the ROMANTIC tradition. The requirements of his apprenticeship as an engraver led to an interest in church Gothic design and architecture, which inspired his love of precise line and pattern. From 1779 he studied at the Royal Academy, and in the 1780s began to publish his own poems with handwritten text and drawings engraved on one plate in a new colour printing technique. He painted in watercolour or tempera, and never painted in oils. The great feature of his work is the power of his visionary imagination. He held that art, imagination and spiritual belief were interrelated, and this mysticism characterizes all his work. His first engraved "illustrated poem" was *Songs of Innocence* (1789), and his longest mystical work is *Jerusalem* (1804-20). He held a one-man exhibition in 1809 and published *A Descriptive Catalogue*, in which he outlined his philosophy on art. In the last decade of his life he was patronized by John Linnell, and during this time he worked on engravings for the *Book of Job* and his magnificent illustration of Dante's *Divine Comedy*. He was the source of inspiration for The ANCIENTS, a group of admirers that included Samuel PALMER, and he has been considered a forerunner of ART NOUVEAU.

Blakelock, Ralph Albert (1847-1919) American painter.

He was self-taught, and his ROMANTIC landscapes are dramatically lit and imbued with a sense of melancholy. His studies of Indians of the Far West were unappreciated in his native New York, and by the time his paintings had achieved recognition and popularity, Blakelock had been committed to an asylum for the insane. Representative works include *Indian Encampment and Pipe Dance* (1872) and *Moonlight Sonata* (1892).

Blaue Reiter, Der The name, taken from a painting by KANDINSKY, of a group of German EXPRESSIONISTS formed in Munich in 1911. Leading members of the group were Kandinsky, MARC, MACKE, KLEE and JAWLENSKY, who, although their working styles were diverse, were united by a philosophy of the creative spirit in European contemporary art. They organized two touring exhibitions in Germany in 1911 and 1912 and produced an *Almanac* (1912), which included major European avante-garde artists as well as tribal, folk and children's art. The idea of the *Almanac* was to unite music, art and literature in a single creative venture. It was intended to be the first in a series, but the group disbanded in 1914.

Blume, Peter (1906-) Russian-born American painter, who studied at the Art Students League in New York. He used the imagery of Surrealism in a precise and meticulous style, and his work is concerned with the communication of ideas through storytelling. His most famous work is *The Eternal City* (1934-7), a satirical attack on the Fascist movement.

Boccioni, Umberto (1882-1916) Italian FUTURIST painter
and sculptor, he wrote *The Technical Mani-festo of Futurist Painting* (1910) and *The Manifesto of Futurist
Sculpture* (1912). One of his early and most important
paintings is *The City Rises* (1910), but from 1912, under
the influence of CUBISM, he developed a richer, semi-abstract style attempting to depict movement, as in *Dynamism of a Cyclist* (1913). A principal sculpture on the
same theme is *Unique Forms of Continuity in Space*
(1913). Boccioni died after a fall from a horse during
World War I.

Böcklin, Arnold (1827-1901) Swiss painter. He studied
in Dusseldorf and Geneva and established his reputation
with the mural *Pan in the Reeds* (1875). His work is
characterized by his use of mythological creatures to
create a symbolic ima-gery relating to primeval human
fears and emotions. Notable works include the five versions of *The Island of the Dead* (from 1880) and a staircase fresco (1868) in the Basel Kunstmuseum, which
also houses a fine collection of his work. He had some
influence on the Surrealist imagery of the 20th century.

body paint *see* **gouache**.

Bologna, Giovanni *or* **Giambologna** (1529-1608) Flemish-born Italian sculptor in the MANNERIST tradition. His
earliest important work is the bronze *Fountain of Neptune* in Bologna (1563-6), a commission by Pope Pius
IV, but he is best known for his popular *Flying Mercury*
and *The Rape of the Sabines* (1583), both in Florence.

Bomberg, David (1890-1957) English painter who studied at the Slade School of Art in London. His early work was highly abstract, as in *The Mud Bath* (1914). He had one-man shows in 1914 and 1919, and the lack of success of the latter forced him into a period of travel and work in isolation. He later abandoned abstraction for a more personal EXPRESSIONIST style. The value of this later work was not appreciated publicly until after his death, but he is now considered one of the pioneers of British expressionism and an influence on AUERBACH.

Bonington, Richard Parkes (1802-28) English painter. He lived in France from 1817 and was a pupil of GROS in Paris, where he became a close friend of DELACROIX. He was a first-class watercolourist, noted for the lightness and fluidity of his style. Along with CONSTABLE, whose work was shown in an exhibition alongside Bonington's at the "English" Salon in 1824, he became a strong influence on the BARBIZON SCHOOL as well as on Delacroix.

Bonnard, Pierre (1867-1947) French IMPRESSIONIST painter, a member of the NABI group in Paris and a founder member of the Salon d'Automne. With the Nabis, he was influenced by GAUGUIN and Japanese art, and designed posters, stained glass and decorative panels. In stage decor he worked on *Ubu Roi* in 1896, and in the early 1900s he painted mainly landscapes. In 1915 a revision of his working style led him to reappraise his attitude to the study of form and composition, which he felt he had hitherto subordinated to a love of colour. He was elected a member of the London Royal Academy in 1940, and retrospective exhibitions of his work were held in 1947 in Paris and in 1966 at the Royal Academy.

Bordone, Paris (1500-71) Italian painter. He worked and studied in Venice from 1510 and was a pupil of TITIAN. In his day, his work was extremely popular and widely acclaimed for its use of chiaro-scuro and vibrant colour. Notable works are the *Presentation of the Ring of St Mark to the Doge* (1538) and *Portrait of a Young Lady* (*c*.1550).

Borduas, Paul Emile (1905-60) Canadian painter. He trained as a church decorator in Montreal and studied in Paris, his early work showing the influence of FAUVISM and SURREALISM. From 1933 he taught in Montreal until the publication of his *Refus Global* manifesto in 1948 aroused the wrath of the established Catholic Church and lost him his job. In the same year he formed the **Automatistes** with a group of young painters whose ideas were based on the spontaneity of creativity. During the 1950s he moved to New York and also held several one-man shows in different parts of the world. His later work was influenced by POLLOCK and RIOPELLE. Notable works include *Sous le Vent de l'Ile* (1947), *Floraison Massive* (1951), *Pulsation* (1955) and *The Seagull* (1957). A major exhibition, *Borduas et les Automatistes*, was held in Paris and Montreal during 1971.

Borglum, Gutzon (1867-1941) American sculptor famous for the portraits, at Mount Rushmore in South Dakota, of American Presidents Washington, Jefferson, Lincoln and Theodore Roosevelt. This massive feat of engineering began in 1930 and was not finished until after the artist's death. A monument to the Confederate Army was begun on Stone Mountain in Georgia but was never finished.

Bosch, Hieronymus [Jerome van Aeken] (*c*.1450-1516) Dutch painter, who took his name from the town of s'Hertogenbosch, where he lived and worked. Of his 40 surviving paintings, none is dated, which makes outlining his development difficult. More conventional paintings, such as the *Crucifixion* in the Musées Royaux in Brussels, may be early works or they may in some cases be commissions. His best-known and most intriguing works are bizarre and confusing, as in *The Garden of Earthly Delights*. His imagery is drawn from religious or moral allegories, folk tales and legends, but his imaginative use of the fantastic and grotesque is so strongly individualistic as to defy understanding. His work was collected by Philip II of Spain, and much of it is in the Prado Museum, Madrid. His influence reached from BRUEGEL in the mid-16th century to 20th-century SURREALISM.

Botticelli, Sandro (1445-1510) Florentine painter who studied under Filippo LIPPI and was influenced by VERROCCHIO. His earliest known commissioned work; in

1470, is a painted panel representing *Fortitude*, and his best-known example from this period is the *Adoration of The Magi*. By 1480 he had his own studio with assistants, and during 1481-82 he worked on the *Moses* and *Christ* frescoes in the Sistine Chapel, Rome. *The Madonna of the Magnificat* (1480s), his best-known altarpiece, is one of several Virgin and Child paintings. He also did a series of mythological paintings for the Medici family, the most famous of which are *Primavera* and *The Birth of Venus* (1482-4). His early style is linear and graceful with elements of Gothic ornamentation, but in the 1490s his work became more dramatic and emotional, as in the intensity of *Pietà*, or the ecstasy of *Mystic Nativity* (1500). By the time of his death his popularity had declined, and his reputation was restored only in the late 19th century through the admiration of the PRE-RAPHAELITES and the esteem in which his work was held by RUSKIN.

Boucher, François (1703-70) French ROCOCO painter who trained as an engraver and was an associate of WATTEAU. In 1723 he took first prize at the Academy and became a member in 1734. From 1727 he was in Rome and was influenced by TIEPOLO. He became a leading interior designer and worked on the royal palace at Versailles as well as designing stage sets and costume details for the Paris Opera. From 1755 he was director of Gobelin's tapestry factory, and in 1765 he became court painter to Louis XV. Madame de Pompadour, of whom he painted several portraits, was one of his patrons. His work was elegant and frivolous, and he treated traditional mythological scenes with wit and humour. Accused by his critics of artificiality and a lack of originality, he responded that he never worked directly from nature because it was "too green, and badly lit." Notable among his works are *The Triumph of Venus* (1740), *The Reclining Girl* (1751) and *The Rising* and *The Setting of the Sun* (1753). FRAGONARD was his pupil.

Boudin, Eugene (1824-98) French painter from Le Havre, where he had a stationery and picture framing business. He always painted directly from nature, mainly beaches, skies and seascapes, and his light, spontaneous brushwork had a strong influence on the IMPRESSIONISTS; MONET and COROT were among his friends and customers who encouraged his painting. Some of his work was hung in the first Impressionist exhibition in 1874.

Bourdelle, Emile Antoine (1861-1929) French sculptor who studied at Toulouse and, after moving to Paris in 1884, exhibited at the Salon des Artistes Françaises. From 1896 he worked under RODIN, and his work up until about 1910 reflects Rodin's Romantic expressiveness. After this period, he developed a more classical style and worked relief sections of the Theatre des Champs Elysees. Notable among his works are the several versions of *Beethoven, Tragic Mask* and the statue *Meracles Archer* (1910). A retrospective exhibition was held in 1928.

Bouts, Dieric (*d.*1475) Dutch painter from Haarlem, who lived and worked mainly in Louvain. His first major commission was an altarpiece for St Peter's Church there. Although influenced by van der WEYDEN and **Albert van Ouwater** (*fl.* 1450s-70s), a Dutch landscape artist, his style is distinctive in its use of perspective, controlled composition, richness of colour and lyrical treatment of landscape. Notable works include *The Last Supper* from the Louvain altarpiece and *The Justice of Emperor Otto*. His treatment of themes such as *Mater Dolorosa* were popular and much copied.

Bramante, Donate (1444-1514) Italian architect and painter, who was a leading and influential architect of the high RENAISSANCE, although the beginnings of his career were centred on painting. His *Men at Arms* frescoes (1480-5), now in the Brera in Milan, and the *Philosophers of the Palazzo del Podista* are examples of early works, and he is thought to have had an influence on Milanese painting. He designed the new St Peter's in Rome, although his plans were modified in the building. RAPHAEL was his pupil, and portrayed him as Euclid in *The School of Athens*.

Brancusi, Constantin (1876-1957) Romanian-born French sculptor, who trained at Crajaua and Bucharest before moving to Paris in 1904, where he met RODIN and worked briefly with MODIGLIANI. Influenced by the woodworking tradition of his native Romania and by the primitivist works of DERAIN and GAUGUIN, he abandoned modelling techniques in favour of direct carving, Working in marble, limestone and, later, in metals and wood, he allowed the materials to lead his craftsmanship and evolved a style of reduction of human and organic forms, as in *Sleeping Muse* (1910) and *The Seal* (1936). He made sculptures for the park at Tiju Jiu in Romania, including the huge *Endless Column* (1937). The essential simplicity of his style, his excellent craftsmanship and sensitivity to materials made him one of the most influential and well-respected sculptors of the 20th century.

Braque, Georges (1882-1963) French painter and, along with PICASSO, one of the founders of CUBISM. He was influenced by the FAUVES' use of colour in his early work, and in 1906 he saw and was impressed by the paintings of CÉZANNE.In 1907 he met Picasso and worked closely with him developing COLLAGE techniques in painting and introducing stencilled lettering, which emphasized the flatness of the picture plane. He was mobilized in 1914 in World War I and was severely wounded in 1917. His subsequent work concentrated on the classical traditions of still life, using his own unique structural methods. Later pieces show a broader handling of paint, elegance of pattern and restrained use of colour. Typical of his work are his series paintings of *Still Lifes* (1920s), *Atelier* (1948-50) and *Oiseaux* (19508).

Breton, André *see* **Surrealism**

Brooks, James (1906-) American painter who studied at

Dallas and at the Art Students' League in New York. He worked as an artist-reporter during World War II, and his work in the 1930s with the Federal Arts Project was a colourful, monumental realism that developed into AB-STRACT EXPRESSIONISM during the 1940s. He turned to AC-TION PAINTING in the 1950s and exhibited with others at the Peridot Gallery. A retrospective show of his work was in the Whitney Museum of American Art during 1963-4.

Brouwer, Adriaen (*c*.1605-38) Flemish painter who was a pupil of Frans HALS at Haarlem. His earliest work is richly coloured in the style of Flemish art. In 1631 he moved to Antwerp, and his palette took on the mono-chromatic tones associated with Dutch painting of the time. Brouwer provides an important link between the two traditions, and his humorous, low-life genre painting was much imitated, although his excellent characteriza-tion and brushwork was never matched. *The Smokers* (*c*.1637) and *The Five Senses* are representative of his work, which was collected by both RUBENS and REMBRANDT

Brown, Ford Madox (1821-93) English painter born in Calais. He studied at Antwerp, Paris and Rome before settling in England in 1845. His early work is ROMANTIC, as in *Execution of Mary, Queen of Scots* (1841), but his links with the PRE-RAPHAELITES led to a development of his painting in this style in his *Chaucer at the Court of Edward III* (1851). His best-known picture is *The Last of*

England (1855) and his most detailed piece, entitled
Work (1863), took eleven years to complete. He also designed glass and furniture for the William MORRIS Company.

Brücke, Die [The Bridge] An association of German artists founded in 1905 in Dresden by KIRCHNER and others.
The name derives from Nietszche's idea that a man can
be seen as a bridge towards a better future, and in this the
artists saw themselves as a link with the art of the future,
in a move away from realism and IMPRESSIONISM. They
also wanted to integrate art and life and so lived together
in community in the tradition of the medieval guilds system. Their influences included African tribal art and the
works of van GOGH and FAUVISM. Their painting was
mainly EXPRESSIONIST, although comprehending a variety
of styles and techniques. They concentrated initially on
figures in landscape and portrait, and made use of texture, clashing colour and aggressive distortion to powerful effect. With Emile NOLDE, they founded the Neue
SEZESSION in 1910, a protest against the refusal of Nolde's
Pentecost by the Berlin Sezession. Members of Die
Brücke then split away from the Neue Sezession and exhibited as a group with the BLAUE REITER. In 1913 the
group disbanded because of conflicts over aims and poli-
cies in relation to the development of CUBISM.

Bruegel *or* **Brueghel, Pieter the Elder** (*c.*1525-69)
Flemish painter and draughtsman and father of Pieter
BREUGHEL [THE YOUNGER] and Jan BRUEGHEL. A promi-

nent figure in Flemish art in the mid-16th century, he rated alongside van EYCK and RUBENS. Bruegel studied under Pieter Coeck van Aelst and later married his tutor's daughter. In 1551 he joined the Antwerp Guild before travelling to France and Italy. More influenced by landscape than southern art, his drawings of the Alps demonstrate his sensitivity to detail and his vision of space, which dominated his subsequent landscape paintings. His print drawings for James Cock in 1555 included such intriguing and detailed drawings as *Big Fish eat Little Fish*, which shows the influence of BOSCH. Paintings in this style include *The Fall of the Rebel Angels* and *The Triumph of Death*. He later moved to Brussels and was commissioned in 1565 by Nicholaes Jonghelsch for *The Months*, a series of paintings that included the famous *Hunters in the Snow*. This particular painting represents an important development in the form of landscape painting. His philanthropic and tolerant view of humanity is ably depicted in his paintings of rustic festivities and proverbial themes, such as *Peasant Wedding Dance* (1566) and *The Misanthrope* (1568). Only about 50 of his paintings survive, but he remains one of the world's most admired and outstanding painters.

Brueghel, Jan (1568-1625) Flemish painter, also called "Velvet" Brueghel, son of Pieter BRUEGEL THE ELDER. He was trained by Mayeken Verhulst, his grandmother, and patronized by Cardinal Borromeo in his travels to Italy from 1594-96. He became Dean of the Antwerp Guild in 1602. He painted mainly landscapes and still lifes, particularly flowers, which were richly coloured and detailed. His landscape work was often of wooded scenes peopled with mythological characters or coaches and horses, usually on small canvases. He collaborated with other artists, including RUBENS, with whom he painted the *Garden of Eden*. David SEGHERS was among his pupils.

Brueghel, Pieter the Younger (1564-1638) Flemish painter, also called "Hell" Brueghel, son of Pieter BRUEGEL THE ELDER. He studied with Gillis van Coninxloo in the Antwerp Guild in 1585. Much of his work involved some copying of his father's works, which provided a source for his own compositions. He had a penchant for scenes of fire and brimstone, as in *The Burning of Troy,* and his work in general is of high quality.

Brunelleschi, Filippo (1377-1446) Italian sculptor and architect. He was a leading figure among the group of RENAISSANCE artists in Florence that included DONATELLO and ALBERTI. He trained initially as a goldsmith, and his earliest extant sculptures are of silver figures, dating from 1398-1400, in Pistoia Cathedral. In 1402 he was defeated by GHIBERTI in a competition to design new doors for the baptistry in Florence Cathedral; each of their entries is now in the Bargello, Florence. His subsequent achievements were mainly in the field of architecture. A major project was building the dome of Florence Cathedral. A later sculptural masterpiece is his painted wooden *Crucifix* 1412) in the church of Santa Maria Novella. He also made major contributions to the development of perspective.

bronze A metal alloy of bronze mixed with tin and occasionally lead and zinc, which has been used as a medium for sculpture since ancient times, when it was cast solid using wooden models. Modern techniques use hollow casting methods of sand casting or *cire perdue* ("lost wax").

brushwork The "handwriting" of a painter, i.e. the distinctive way in which he or she applies paint, either smoothly or roughly, thinly or thickly, in long strokes or short. Like handwriting, brushwork is individual to a painter.

Buffet, Bernard (1928-) French painter. He studied at the Ecole des Beaux-Arts in 1944, and in 1948 he shared the Prix de la Critique. He was a member of the Homme-Témoin group, and by the 1950s had held several successful exhibitions at the Drouant-David gallery. His distinctive linear style was popular and much admired by younger artists. The pessimistic atmosphere of his solitary, emaciated figures and distorted still lifes painted from a restrained and neutral palette seems to capture a sense of postwar futility that had great popular appeal. His later work has been criticized for its formularity and slickness.

Buonarotti, Michaelangelo *see* **Michaelangelo Buonarotti**

Buonisegna, Duccio de *see* **Duccio di Buonisegna**

Burchfield, Charles (1893-1967) American painter from Ohio, who studied at Cleveland Museum School of Art. During his early career he suffered from bouts of depression and obsessive fears that are reflected in work from this period, as in *Church Bells Ringing, Rainy Winter Night* (1917) and *Noontide in Late May* (1917). During the 1920s and 30s his style became more documentary, although still retaining a sense of strangeness in perspective, as in *November Evening* (1934). His later work is more mystical and atmospheric, as in *Sun and Rocks* (1950).

Burne-Jones, Sir Edward Coley (1833-98) English painter, designer and illustrator. He studied at Oxford University, where he met William MORRIS, who first interested him in art, and Dante Gabriel ROSSETTI, who remained a major influence on his style. He began to exhibit in 1877 and quickly became popular. From 1885-93 his work dwelt on escapist themes of myth and legend, imbued with a dreamlike, unreal quality of his own imagination. His later work was influenced by BOTTICELLI, especially in his portrayal of female beauty. He also designed tapestries and stained glass for William Morris's company.

Butler, Reg (1913-81) British sculptor, who originally trained in architecture, which he practised up until 1950.

He began making sculptures, as an assistant to Henry MOORE, from 1947. A conscientious objector in World War II, he worked as a blacksmith and later made use of this experience in his welding techniques and metal sculptures, such as *The Birdcage* (1951). He rose to fame in 1953 after winning a competition for a monument to the *Unknown Political Prisoner*. His early style was fairly abstract, but later work is more figurative and sensuous.

C

Cadell, Francis Campbell Boileau (1883-1937) Scottish painter. He was influenced by CÉZANNE and by POST-IMPRESSIONIST art, and from around 1910 he gradually developed his own colourist style. A friend and contemporary of PEPLOE, he went regularly to the island of Iona during the 1920s and 1930s, painting bold, clearly coloured landscapes in a geometrically simplified style. *Interior–The Orange Blind* (*c.* 1928) is typical of his non-landscape works.

Calder, Alexander (1898-1976) American sculptor famous for his moving sculptures, or '"mobiles"; non-moving ones he called"stabiles." Originally trained as an engineer, he began sculpting in wel-ded metal in his mid-twenties. Early work consisted of portraits and animated toys in wood and metal, e.g. *The Brass Family* (1929). These were brightly coloured and organic, in a form suggestive of SURREALISM. His first exhibition was held in 1932 and thereafter he exhibited worldwide. Other notable works are *A Universe* (1934), *Mobile* (1958) and *The City* (1960).

Caliari, Paolo *see* **Veronese, Paolo**.

Campin, Robert (*c.* 1378-1444) Flemish painter, also

known as the Master of Flemalle. Little is known of his real identity or the extent of his work. Two dated works are the wings of the *Welde* altarpiece (1438), now in the Prado, Madrid, and a painted stone *Annunciation* (1428). Another probable piece is a triptych, *The Entombment* (*c*.1415-20). He may also have been a teacher of Rogier van der WEYDEN, and his development of perspective and chiaroscuro techniques had a considerable influence on the beginnings of the Netherlandish School.

Canaletto, Giovanni Antonio Canal (1697-1768) Venetian painter who studied under Panini in Rome but worked in Venice, apart from a ten-year period in England. An unrivalled architectural painter with an excellent sense of composition, he was commercially successful due to the efforts of Joseph Smith, an English businesman who marketed his work for the tourist trade. Canaletto was a prolific and innovative artist, producing numerous drawings and etchings, not as preparatory sketches but as finished works in themselves. Smith also bought a large collection of his paintings, which he later sold to George III of England and much of this is still in the Royal Collection. Notable works include *The Stone-mason's Yard* (*c*.1730) and *View of the Grand Canal.*

Canova, Antonio (1757-1822) Italian sculptor. His earliest work is naturalistic and emotional, as in *Daedalus and Icarus* (1779), but his first important commission, for the tomb of Pope Clement XIV (1783-7), shows the calm restraint and graceful contours that led to his becoming one of the major NEOCLASSICAL sculptors of the 18th century. Among his portrait sculptures are the *Emperor Napoleon I* and his sister, *Paulina Borghese*. Canova's consid-erable talent was out of fashion during the ROMANTIC period and has only subsequently achieved acclaim.

Caravaggio, Michaelangelo Amerighi da (1573-1610) Italian painter from Milan, who worked in Rome from 1592. His earliest paintings were small commissions, such as the *Music Party,* sharply focussed but less dramatic than his mature work. The strong, bold, expressive use of light with which he made the technique of chiaroscuro his own is evident first in such works as *The Life of St Matthew* (1599-1602) and the *Crucifixion of St Peter* (1600-1608). After 1600 he painted only religious subjects, portraying ordinary people as Biblical characters, and working directly on to the canvas, to the horror of his religious patrons and his critics respectively. Initial versions of *St Matthew and the Angel*, the *Crucifixion of St Peter* and *The Conversion of St Paul*, all refused by the church authorities, were bought by Vincenzo Giustiniani. Caravaggio fled Rome in 1606 after killing a man in a fight, but his paintings from the last four years of his life include some remarkable works, notably the famous *Beheading of John the Baptist*. Caravaggio died of malaria, aged 37.

caricature A drawing of a person in which his or her most prominent features are exaggerated or distorted in order to produce a recognizable but ridiculous portrait, possibly suggesting a likeness to another object. The technique was pioneered by Annibale CARRACCI in the late 16th century and flourished in the 18th and 19th centuries through the work of painters such as HOGARTH and the caricaturists ROWLANDSON and DAUMIER.

Caro, Anthony (1924-) British sculptor. Originally trained as an engineer, he was an assistant to Henry MOORE from 1951-53. Influenced by DE KOONING and DUBUFFET, his early work is simplistic in form with an emphasis on surface texture. Later sculptures are prefabricated pieces of metal bolted or welded together and then painted, as in *Midday* (1960). His mature work shows a renewed interest in rusted and weathered materials. Caro has had a considerable influence on younger sculptors.

cartoon (1) A drawing, or series of drawings, intended to convey humour, satire or wit. Cartoons were commonly used from the 18th century onwards in newspapers and periodicals as a vehicle for social and political comment, and in comic magazines for children and adults in the 20th century. (2) A full-size preparatory drawing for a painting, mural or fresco. The drawing was fully worked out on paper and then mapped out on to the surface to be painted.

Carpaccio, Vittore (*c.*1450-1525) Venetian painter. His style shows the influence of Gentile BELLINI, in the series of paintings on *Scenes from the Life of St Ursula*

(1490s). His sense of detail and command of perspective are evident in *St George Killing the Dragon,* as are his delicate and graceful use of light. He was a popular painter in his own day, and in the 19th century with the critic John RUSKIN. A notable favourite is *Two Courtesans,* a fragment of a larger painting, which was much copied.

Carpeaux, Jean-Baptiste (1827-75) French sculptor and painter. He won the Prix de Rome in 1854 and returned to Paris where he became a court favourite. He was commissioned for several portrait busts and also sculpted large groups, such as La *Danse* for the Opera and the relief *Flora* at the Tuileries. His work was expressive and emotional and represented a move away from neoclassical trends. He influenced RODIN. Notable works include *Neapolitan Fisherboy* (1858) and *Ugolino* (1860).

Carrà, Carlo (1881-1966) Italian painter. An advocate of FUTURISM (he wrote his own manifesto in 1913), he broke away from it in 1915 when he and de CHIRICO founded METAPHYSICAL PAINTING.

Carracci, Annibale (1560-1609) Bolognese painter, a brother of **Agostin**o (1560-1608) and cousin of **Ludovico** (1555-1619), together with whom he founded a teaching academy in 1585. Their teaching concentrated on realistic representation of form drawn direct from nature, inspiring a new generation of Italian painters and forming the beginnings of the High RENAISSANCE in the 1600s. DOMENICO and RENI were among their pupils. Annibale, famous as the father of modern CARICATURE, rated alongside CARAVAGGIO in greatness and achievement. His early style of genre painting is direct and lively, as in *The Butcher's Shop* (*c*.1582). His work on the ceilings of the Farnese Palace in Rome (1597-1600), based on sources in antique sculpture, influenced early BAROQUE painting, and the treatment of landscape in his *Flight into Egypt* (*c*.1604) influenced the work of CLAUDE and POUSSIN. His brother Agostino was an engraver whose studies of the human body, published after his death, were used in teaching for the next two centuries. Like Annibale, he was a brilliant draughtsman and an important teacher at the Carracci Academy. Ludovico's style of work was much more painterly than that of his cousins, and he remained the driving force at the academy after the others had moved to Rome. His representations of light and texture influenced his pupil GUERNICO.

Carucci, Jacopo *see* **Pontormo.**

Cassat, Mary (1845-1926) American painter, who lived and worked mainly in Paris, where she was associated with the IMPRESSIONISTS, particularly DEGAS, MONET and COURBET. Her draughtsmanship was excellent and her sense of design influenced by Japanese art. Notable works include *Lady at the Tea Table* (1885) and *Gathering Fruit* (1892). *Mère et Enfant* (1905) is representative of a favourite subject in her later career.

Castagno, Andrea del *see* **Andrea del Castagno.**

Catlin, George (1796-1824) American painter, who was

a lawyer before taking up painting in 1821. A self-taught artist, he painted portraits including over 500 of American Indians, among whom he lived from 1830-36. These were unappreciated in the US but their colourful directness was much praised when they were taken to France and England.

Cave Paintings *see* **Altamira; Lascaux.**

Cellini, Benvenuto (1500-71) Florentine MANNERIST sculptor and goldsmith. He made jewellery and medals to Papal commissions in his early career, but little of this has survived. In France in the 1540s he made a famous salt cellar with the gold and enamel figures of *Neptune and Ceres*, and he learned bronze-casting there, returning to Florence to create the great masterpiece of Mannerist sculpture, *Perseus* (1554), commissioned by Duke Cosimo Medici I. He also wrote a famous autobiography, which was found and published in 1728.

Cézanne, Paul (1839-1906) French painter. He studied in Paris, where he met PISSARRO, who was to become a lifelong friend, and the Impressionists MONET and RENOIR. Cézanne's early work, influenced by DELACROIX, was ROMANTIC in style, but from the late 1860s he introduced restraining discipline to his work and began painting directly from nature. He was more interested in form and structure than in the light effects that inspired IMPRESSIONISM. Notable works are views of *Mont Ste Victoire* and *L'Estaque* . He had a one-man show in 1875 and a retrospective was held in 1907. His work had a huge influence on CUBISM and 20th-century art generally.

Chadwick, Lynn (1914-) British sculptor, who experimented with "balancing sculptures" and mobiles in welded iron, inspired by animal and insect forms. He has had international acclaim and won the Sculpture Prize at the 28th Venice Bienniale. A retrospective exhibition was held in 1957.

Chagall, Marc (1887-1985) Russian-born French painter, who studied with BAKST in St Petersburg before moving to Paris in 1910, where he met MODIGLIANI, and DELAUNAY. His style suggests the influences of CUBISM and ORPHISM, but his unique, juxtaposed imagery is drawn from his own childhood memories. A notable early work is *Land the Village* (1911). He returned to Russia in 1914 and taught for a time, but found himself out of step with socialist-realist trends and from 1923 he moved between France and the US, teaching, illustrating books and designing stage sets and stained glass.

chalk A soft stone, similar to a very soft limestone, used for drawing. **Crayon** is powdered chalk mixed with oil or wax.

Champaigne, Philippe de (1602-74) Flemish-born French painter whose patrons included Queen Marie de Medici and Cardinal Richelieu. He was a successful portrait painter and also worked on frescoes at the Sorbonne and decoration for the Palais Royale in Paris. From 1643-64, he produced some of his best work, its simplistic austerity influenced by Jansenist thought, e.g. *Ex*

Voto (1662). This painting marks his daughter's miraculous cure from paralysis through the prayers of her fellow nuns at the convent of Port-Royale.

charcoal The carbon residue from wood that has been partially burned. Charcoal will make easily erasable black marks and is used mainly to make preliminary drawings, e.g. on walls. When used on paper it has to be coated with a fixative to make the drawing permanent.

Chardin, Jean-Baptiste Simeon (1699-1779) French painter, who became a member of the French Academy in 1728. Compared with the fashionable ROCOCO of contemporaries like BOUCHER, Chardin's small-scale genre paintings and still lifes were realistically direct and natural, as in *Rayfish, Cat and Kitchen Utensils* (1728). He later turned to pastel drawing because of failing eyesight and produced various portraits of himself and his wife. FRAGONARD was his pupil.

Chavannes, Puvis de *see* **Puvis de Chavannes.**

chiaroscuro An Italian word (literally "light-dark") used to describe the treatment of light and shade in a painting, drawing or engraving to convey depth and shape. It is particularly used of works by painters like CARAVAGGIO or REMBRANDT.

Chinoiserie 16th and 17th century trade with the Far East created a European market for Chinese art and influenced the development of a vogue for things Chinese. Pagodas and stylized scenes, plants and animals conceived to be in the Chinese style began to decorate pottery, furniture, fabrics and ornaments. These were finally mass-produced, both in Europe and the Far East, specifically for this market. A familiar product in this style is the famous Willow Pattern pottery range.

Chirico, Giorgio de (1888-1978) Greek-born Italian painter. He exhibited his series of "enigmatic" pictures in Paris in 1911. These are characterized by figures or statues in a townscape of strange perspectives and unnatural shadows. During World War I he was posted to Ferrara in Italy, where he met CARRÀ, with whom he founded META-PHYSICAL PAINTING. He later came to be seen as a forerunner of SURREALISM, but he himself abandoned modern art in the 1930s in favour of the tradition of the "Old Masters".

Christo Javacheff (1935-   ) Bulgarian-born American sculptor, who studied in Sofia and Vienna and was a member of the Nouveaux Realités group in Paris from 1958. He settled in Chicago in 1964 and continued his experiments with ASSEMBLAGE and "packaging." His initial "wrapped" objects were small in scale and intended to draw attention to the ambiguity of ordinary objects when parcelled up. He went on to wrap cars, trees, famous buildings, such as the Reichstag in Berlin, and areas of landscape e.g. *Valley Curtain* in Colorado.

Church, Frederick Edwin (1826-1900) American painter, who studied under COLE, from whom he absorbed a sense of the grandeur of nature. He painted huge epic works based on sketches of South American scenery, e.g. *The Heart of the Andes* (1859). He also travelled Europe and Asia, and his most famous work, the *Falls of Niagara* (1857), was a huge success at the Paris Exhibition in 1867.

Churriguera, José Benito (1665-1725) Spanish sculptor and architect and prominent member of a family of artists famous for their ornate designs for church sculptures and altarpieces. He worked in Salamanca, where he built the high altar of the Church of San Estaban, and also in Madrid. The term *Churrigueresque* refers to any elaborate decoration of Spanish BAROQUE.

Cimabue [Cenni de Peppi] (*c*.1272-1302) Florentine painter. Possibly a teacher of GIOTTO, he is mentioned in Dante's *Divine Comedy* as being "eclipsed by Giotto's fame," but there is little documented evidence of his life and work. Part of a mosaic in Pisa Cathedral is known to be his work, and various others have been attributed to him, including the *Madonna of Santa Trinità* in the Uffizi in Florence.

cinquecento The Italian term for the 16th century.

classicism A style of art based on order, serenity and emotional control, with reference to the classical art of the ancient Greeks and Romans. It eschews the impulsive creativity and sponteneity of ROMANTICISM in favour of peace, harmony and strict ideals of beauty. Figures drawn in the classsical style were usually symmetrical and devoid of the normal irregularities of nature. *See also* NEOCLASSICISM.

Claude Gellée, called **Claude Lorraine** (1600-82) French painter who studied in France before settling in Rome in 1627. Early works were influenced by the MANNERISTS, e.g. ELSHEIMER, but, drawing from nature with great sensitivity to light, his style matured into a harmonious CLASSICISM. His pastoral landscapes were so popular that he produced a sketchbook of his paintings, *Liber Veritatis*, to guard against forgeries. He had a tremendous influence on 17th and 18th century landscape painters. Notable works include *Landscape at Sunset* (1639) and *The Expulsion of Hagar* (1668).

Close, Chuck (1940) American painter and pioneer of "Superrealism" as a reaction against the strong emotions of ABSTRACT EXPRESSIONISM. His work involves projecting photographic images, usually portraits, on to a grid-patterned canvas that is then airbrushed in, a square at a time. These take months to complete and are representative of the Superrealist avoidance of painterly techniques.

Clouet, François (*c.*1510-72) French painter, son of Jean, or Janet, CLOUET. He was appointed court painter in 1541 and is thought to have painted the famous *King Francis I* (1542). His influences included the MANNERISTS, e.g. Pontormo. His excellence as a portraitist can be seen in his collection of drawings in the Musée Condé at Chantilly, and in his earliest signed portrait of *Pierre Quthe* (1562). Another notable work is *Lady in her Path* (*c.*1570).

Clouet, Jean, *called* **Janet** (*d*.1540/1) French portrait painter and father of Francois CLOUET, who succeeded him as court painter to Francis I. None of his work is signed or documented, and they are attributed to him through a series of drawings thought to be his. These include *The Dauphin Francis* and *Man Holding Petrarch's Works.*

Cole, Thomas (1801-48) English-born American painter, founder of the HUDSON RIVER SCHOOL and pioneer of American landscape painting. He began his career with paintings from sketches of the Hudson River in 1825. Visits to Europe influenced his later depictions of religious and allegorical themes in dramatic settings as in the series paintings, *The Course of Empire* (1838) and *The Voyage of Life* (1840). CHURCH was his pupil.

collage A piece of art created by adhering pieces of paper, fabric, wood, etc, on to a flat surface. The technique was popular with the Cubists, BRAQUE and PICASSO, and is a precursor of the more sculptural methods of ASSEMBLAGE.

colour An effect induced in the eye by light of various wavelengths, the colour perceived depending on the specific wavelength of light reflected by an object. Most objects contain pigments that absorb certain light frequencies and reflect others, e.g. the plant pigment chlorophyll usually absorbs orange or red light and reflects green or blue, therefore the majority of plants appear to be green in colour. A white surface is one where all light frequencies are reflected and a black surface absorbs all frequencies. Artists' colours are made by combining pigments of vegetable or mineral extraction with an appropriate medium, e.g. linseed oil. The rarity of some mineral pigments has a direct effect on the prices of particular colours.

colour field painting a movement begun by ABSTRACT EXPRESSIONISTS including ROTHKO and NOLAN towards a more intellectual abstraction. Their paintings were large areas of pure, flat colour, the mood and atmosphere being created by the shape of the canvas and by sheer scale.

colourist A term in art criticism referring to an artist who places emphasis on colour over line or form. For example, TITIAN and GIORGIONE have been called the "Venetian Colourists." The term is, however, too vague to be applied consistently.

composition The arrangement of elements in a drawing, painting or sculpture in proper proportion and relation to each other and to the whole.

concrete art A term used to describe severely geometrical ABSTRACT ART.

Constable, John (1776-1837) English painter. He studied at the Royal Academy in London and while he admired GAINSBOROUGH and the Dutch landscapists, the main influence on his work was the English countryside. He was an ardent believer in studying nature directly, as demonstrated in *Cloud Studies* (1816-22) and full-size sketches for paintings like *View on the Stour* (1819) and *The Haywain* (1820). Initially less popular in England than in France, he influenced BONINGTON and DELACROIX and the BARBIZON SCHOOL, as well as providing a source of inspiration for the IMPRESSIONISTS. He became a member of the Royal Academy in 1829, and as a result of the death of his wife in the previous year, his mature work became more intense and dramatic, as in *Hadleigh Castle* (1829).

constructivism a movement in ABSTRACT EXPRESSIONISM concerned with forms and movement in sculpture and the aesthetics of the industrial age. It began in post-World War I Russia with the sculptors PEVSNER, GABO and TATLIN. Their work, which made use of modern plastics, glass and wood, was intentionally non-representational. Their ideas were published in Gabo's *Realistic Manifesto* (1920). Gabo and Pevsner left Russia in 1922 and 1923 res-pectively and went on to exert great influence on western art. Tatlin remained to pursue his own ideals of the social and aesthetic usefulness of his art, and in this he was later associated with RODCHENKO.

Cooper, Samuel (1609-72) English painter of miniature portraits. He was an excellent draughtsman, and his distinctive style of BAROQUE composition made his work much sought after. The writer Samuel Pepys is thought to have paid £38 for a miniature of his wife. Cooper also painted slightly larger portraits of *Charles I* and the *First Earl of Shaftesbury*. His brother, **Alexander Cooper** (*d.*1660), although less well known was also a painter of miniatures.

Copley, John Singleton (1738-1815) American painter and one of the greatest portraitists of the 18th century. His reputation was established in Boston during the 1750s and 60s with portraits of famous and professional people, such as Paul Revere and Samuel Adams. He settled in London in 1774 and entered the Royal Academy in 1779. His most popular English works were *Brook Watson and the Shark* (1788) and large dramatic scenes of contemporary events, e.g. *The Death of Chatham* (1780).

Corinth, Lovis (1858-1925) German painter who studied in Paris. His early work shows the in-fluence of Frans HALS and RUBENS. He later developed a baroque style using IMPRESSIONIST techniques, as in *Salomé* (1899). He was elected President of the Berlin SEZESSION in 1911 and had a stroke later that year, which made painting more difficult for him. His subsequent work is more expressionist in style, as in *The Walchsee with a Yellow Field* (1921).

Cornelius, Peter von (1783-1867) German painter who studied at Dusseldorf and in Italy, and joined the NAZARENES in 1811. He was head of the Munich Academy from 1825 and later worked in Berlin. His early style was influenced by medieval art, but his later work owes more to RAPHAEL and MICHELANGELO. He revived German interest in monumental fresco painting, a notable example of which is the *Last Judgement* in the Ludwigskirche in Munich.

Cornell, Joseph (1903-73) American self-taught sculptor and pioneer of ASSEMBLAGE techniques. His best-known works are his shallow, upright boxes containing collaged pictures and small objects like_pieces of Victorian antiques. A typical work is *Medici Slot Machine* (1942). His style is CONSTRUCTIVIST in approach with SURREALIST overtones.

Corot, Jean-Baptiste Camille (1796-1875) French painter. He was encouraged to draw from nature, and was influenced by classical landscape. As a result, some of his earliest work was already ahead of his time in originality, as in *The Farnese Gardens* (1826). He continued to produce highly popular landscapes, some more romantic in feeling than others, e.g. *Memory of Mortfontaine*, and was awarded the Légion d'Honneur in 1846. He greatly influenced landscape painting in the late 19th century.

Correggio, Antonio Allegri da (*d.*1534) Italian painter from Parma, a leading figure of the High RENAISSANCE. His early work suggests influences of MANTEGNA, LEONARDO and RAPHAEL, as in *The Madonna of St Francis* (1515), but it is his fresco work, along with commissions like *Jupiter and Io* (*c.*1530) and *The Rape of Ganymede*, which had the greatest influence on later BAROQUE and ROCOCO painters. In the cupolas of the church of San Giovanni Evangelista and the Cathedral at Parma he painted a central oculus, or illusory skylight, peopled with figures in flight, a technique copied from

Mantegna but with the foreshortening and sense of illusion taken to new levels of ingenuity.

Cotman, John Sell (1782-1842) English draughtsman and painter, who was leader of the Norwich School of English landscape painters from 1806. He is best known for his sepia and watercolour landscapes, such as *Greta Bridge* (1805).

Courbet, Gustave (1819-77) French painter. His early work was Romantic in style, but from the 1850s he became known for a brand of social realism that was as innovative as it was controversial. His large-scale genre paintings, such as *The Stonebreakers* (1850) and *Burial at Ornans* (1851), were criticized as focussing too much on the ugly and distasteful, but these works were important in their deliberate move away from CLASSICAL and ROMANTIC themes, and they influenced the representation of everyday subjects in art. Another notable and controversial piece was *The Artist's Studio* (1855). His later work was less intense and includes more landscape and seascape paintings. A retrospective of Courbet's work was held in 1880.

Cranach, Lucas (1472-1553) German painter, whose early works were dramatic compositions, such as *Crucifixion* (1503) and *Rest on the Flight* (1504), inspired by the wooded landscape of the Danube around Vienna. He became court painter to the Elector of Saxony and painted portraits of classical subjects like *Apollo and Diana* (1530). He also designed woodcut prints for the

Protestant cause, as well as painting a number of portraits of Martin Luther.

Crawford, Thomas (1814-57) American sculptor in the NEOCLASSICAL tradition. He lived and worked mainly in Rome, where he designed the famous bronze Ar*med Liberty* (1863) for the dome of the Capitol in Washington.

crayon *see* **chalk.**

Cronaca, Il, *see* **Pollaiuolo, Antonio del**.

Cubism An art movement started by PICASSO and BRAQUE and influenced by African tribal masks and carvings and by the work of CÉZANNE. They moved away from realist and impressionist trends towards a more intellectual representation of objects. Hitherto, painters had observed subjects from a fixed viewpoint, but the Cubists also wanted to represent a more cerebral understanding of their subject. The result was an explosion of multi-viewpoint images, often broken up into geometric shapes and realigned to suggest faces full on and in profile together, to explain the three-dimensional variety of an object or to imply movement, as in DUCHAMP'S series, *Nude Descending a Staircase*. Such fragmented images could be highly complicated. Cubism had an enormous and continuing influence on 20th-century art, and other notable exponents of the movement were GRIS, LEGER, and DELAUNAY.

Curry, John Steuart (1897-1946) American painter, who trained as an illustrator before starting to paint scenes of American life in the midwest. He worked on the Federal

Arts Project in the 1930s, painting murals that established his reputation as a regionalist painter. His works, influenced by RUBENS, are occasionally over-dramatic. Typical of his work is *Baptism in Kansas* (1928).

Cuyp, Aelbert (1620-91) Dutch landscape painter, the outstanding member of a family of artists from Dordrecht. His work was inspired by the river landscapes of northern Europe, of the Maas and the Rhine, his favourite subjects being fields of cows. He had a strong sense of composition and light, creating warm, still scenes of great dignity and grandeur, e.g. *The Maas at Dordrecht*. His father, **Jacob Gerritz Cuyp** (1594-1651) was principally a painter of portraits, such as *Boy with a Hawk* (1643), while his uncle, **Benjamin Gerritz Cuyp** (1612-52), was a genre painter of Biblical scenes, like *Adoration of the Shepherds*.

D

Dada An art movement that began in Zurich in 1915, its name randomly chosen from a lexicon. Dada represented a reaction to postwar disillusion with established art. Leading figures included Jean ARP and the poet Tristan Tzara, and, when the movement spread to New York, PICABIA and DU-CHAMP. Its aim was to reject accepted aesthetic and cultural values and to promote an irrational form of non-art, or anti-art. The random juxtapositions of COLLAGE and the use of ready-made objects suited their purpose best. A notable example is Duchamp's *Fountain* (1917), which was an unadorned urinal. Dada gave way to NEUE SACHLICHKEIT around 1924 as the artists associated with the movement diversified. It led, however, to the beginnings of SURREALISM and is the source of other movements in ABSTRACT ART, such as "happenings" (*see* BEUYS KAPROW) and ACTION PAINTING.

Daddi, Bernardo (*fl.*1290-1349) Florentine painter, whose earliest documented work is *The Madonna Enthroned* (1328), which shows the influence of his older contemporary GIOTTO. A larger *Madonna* is in the Or San Michele. Daddi's other small panels are happier and more lyrical than the work of Giotto, and his popularity and influence continued into the late 14th century.

Dali, Salvador (1904-89) Spanish painter, whose early
influences included CUBISM and metaphysical painting
before he joined the SURREALISTS in 1928. His work is
precise and academic in execution, giving weight and
emphasis to the hallucinatory neuroses of his subject
matter. Notable works include *Limp Watches* (1931),
The Last Supper (1955), and the famous *Christ of St
John of the Cross* (1951). Although he was expelled
from the Surrealists in 1938, he is popularly thought of
as *the* representative Surrealist painter.

Danube School *see* **Altdorfer, Albrecht**.

Daubigny, Charles François (1817-79) French painter,
member of the BARBIZON SCHOOL and a pioneer of *plein
air* landscape painting. His early work was influenced by
CLAUDE among others, but later paintings have an open
and light atmosphere more associated with Dutch landscape, and these became a source of inspiration to the
IMPRESSIONISTS. He had a studio-boat from which he
painted his favourite river and canal scenes, such as *View
from the Seine* (1852).

Daumier, Honoré (1808-97) French cartoonist, painter
and sculptor, he worked for the Republican magazine
Caricature in which his cartoons depicting King Louis
Philippe as *Gargantua* caused him six months imprison-
ment. After the suppression of *Caricature* he made bourgeois society his target in *Le Charivari*. He was proficient and prolific in the newly developed medium of lithography, producing over 4,000 lithographs in the

course of his career. He was also an original and innovative painter and sculptor. *Washerwoman* is typical of his sympathetic but unsentimental treatment of the pathos of day to day life for the poor. Daumier influenced the works of MILLET and COROT, and he spent his last years, blind and impoverished, in a cottage given to him by the latter.

David, Jacques Louis (1784-1825) French NEOCLASSICAL painter. He won the Prix de Rome in 1775. His earliest work was in the ROCOCO tradition, but a more realistic approach and appreciation of the ANTIQUE are evident in some of his best-known works, e.g. the *Oath of the Horatii* (1784) and *Death of Socrates* (1787). He was the leading artist of the French Revolution and was imprisoned after the death of Robespierre: *View of the Luxembourg Gardens* (1794) was painted at this time. He survived to become painter to Napoleon Bonaparte and painted *The Coronation of Napoleon* (1805-7), but after the Battle of Waterloo he fled to Brussels, where he died in exile. GROS and INGRES were his pupils.

Davie, Alan (1920-) Scottish painter. He studied at Edinburgh School of Art, and early influences include POLLOCK and DE KOONING. His own style of mystical EXPRESSIONISM is vigorous and dynamic. He has held many one-man shows in Europe and the US, and has won many awards, including Best Foreign Painter at the San Paulo Bienniale in 1963.

Davies, Arthur Bowen (1862-1928) American artist,

whose early influences include WHISTLER, BOTTICELLI and PUVIS DE CHAVANNES, as in *Unicorns* (1906), although his later work was more affected by CUBISM. He was a member of The EIGHT and also helped organize the ARMORY SHOW. He later worked on the establishment of the Museum of Modern Art in New York.

Davis, Stuart (1894-1964) American painter, whose early work was influenced by the ARMORY SHOW and the work of LÉGER, as in *Lucky Strike* (1921). He later developed a more precise, hard-edged style, but his mature work is brighter and more decorative, as in *Oah! In Sao Pao* (1951).

Degas, Edgar (1834-1917) French painter and sculptor. He studied at the Ecole des Beaux Arts in Paris, and the Old Masters and Renaissance painters formed his early influences. During the 1860s he met MONET and began exhibiting with the IMPRESSIONISTS, although he was less interested in *plein air* effects of light than in capturing movement or gesture. He is famous for his many paintings and pastel drawings of racehorses and ballet dancers, e.g. *Ballet Rehearsal* (1874). In later life he turned to sculpture because of failing eyesight, although ballet remained a favourite theme, e.g. *The Little Fourteen-year-old Ballet Dancer* (1881). His merits were recognized early, and his achievement has endured. A retrospective exhibition of his work was held in Paris in 1937.

De Kooning, Willem (1904-   ) Dutch-born American painter, a member of the New York School and a major exponent of ABSTRACT EXPRESSIONISM. He came to prominence in the 1940s with his strong, enigmatic paintings of female figures. These subjects and landscapes have dominated most of his work, as in his *Woman* series of the 1950s. He has had widespread influence on the work of other abstract artists.

Delacroix, Eugène (1798-1863) French painter whose early influences included GÉRICAULT and RUBENS. His early work, while ROMANTIC in subject matter, owes much to CLASSICAL composition, as in *The Barque of Dante* (1822). He was a friend of BONINGTON, and with him studied the work of CONSTABLE in England. He also visited North Africa, which inspired works such as *Women of Algiers* (1834). He undertook commissions for murals and portraits, notably of *Paganini* (1832) and *Chopin and George Sand* (1838). He also kept a journal of his work and influenced other artists, particularly those of the BARBIZON SCHOOL.

Delaunay, Robert (1883-1935) French painter and originator of ORPHISM, along with his wife, **Sonia Delaunay-Terk** (1885-1979). His early experiments with CUBISM, NEO-IMPRESSIONISM and FAUVISM combined to influence the development of his style, as in his series paintings of the *Eiffel Tower* (1910) and *Windows. Circular Forms* (1912) was a more abstract development. His work inspired many of the German Expressionists, including MACKE and KLEE.

Demuth, Charles (1883-1935) American painter and leading precisionist artist. His work embraced a variety of styles, and his influences include CÉZANNE and DUCHAMP in paintings such as *Acrobats* (1919) and *Box of Tricks* (1920). He was also a proficient illustrator and his best-known work, based on a poem by William Carlos Williams, is *I Saw the Figure Five in Gold* (1928). Demuth lived and worked mainly in Paris.

Denis, Maurice (1870-1943) French painter and founder member of the NABIS group, he studied at the Atelier Julien, where he met BONNARD and SERUSIER. One of his best-known works, *Hommage à Cézanne* (1900), portrays members of the Nabis. He also founded the *Ateliers d'Art Sacre* and painted frescoes in the Church of St Paul in Geneva, and *Catholic Mystery* (1890). His works in general display a sense of priority of line and colour over realistic representation of form.

Derain, André (1880-1945) French painter, who studied at the Académie Carrière and, along with MATISSE, founded FAUVISM. Van GOGH was an influence in his early work, as in *Mountains at Colliours* (1905), and he was one of the first to be influenced by African tribal art, creating granite masks and block-like figure sculptures. His mature works owe more to CÉZANNE and to RENAISSANCE art, becoming more CLASSICAL in style.

De, Stijl *see* **Stijl, De**

diptych A pair of paintings or carvings on two panels hinged together so that they can be opened or closed.

distemper An impermanent paint made by mixing colours with eggs or glue instead of oil.

Divisionism *see* **Post-Impressionism**.

Dix, Otto (1891-1969) German painter in the social-realist tradition of the NEUE SACHLICHKEIT. His work is meticulously detailed and realistic, his criticism of society undiluted, as in *The City* triptych (1927-8). His expressive use of distortion heightened the ugliness of themes such as *The War* (1923-4). He brought the same direct forcefulness to his portraits, e.g. *Sylvia von Herden* (1926). His work was denounced as degenerate by the Nazis, but he returned to his career after 1945.

Doesburg, Theo van (1883-1931) Dutch painter, founder member of the De STIJL group and editor of its magazine. His early work was influenced by FAUVISM and POST-IMPRESSIONISM, but his style became increasingly abstract under the influence of MONDRIAN, whom he met in 1915. He wrote about, and lectured on, De Stijl, and influenced ideas from the BAUHAUS to modern ABSTRACT ART. Examples of his work include *The Cow* (1916-17) and *Counter-composition in Dissonances no. XVI* (1925).

Domenichino [Domenico Zampiere] (1581-1641) Italian painter and pupil of Annibale CARRACCI, at whose academy in Rome he studied. From 1610 he was the city's leading painter. He painted The *Life of St Cecilia* fresco (1611-14) in the Church of San Luigi dei Francesca, which is CLASSICAL in style, and the BAROQUE *Four Evangelists* (1624-8) in the Church of San Andrea della Valle. His popularity declined after the 1620s, but was revived for a time in the 18th century. Other notable works include *Landscape with Tobias and the Angel* (*c.*1615) and *Last Communion of St Jerome* (1614).

Domenico Veneziano (*c.*1400-1461) Italian painter and contemporary of CASTAGNO, he was influenced by DONATELLO. His best-known surviving work is the *St Lucy* altarpiece (*c.*1445), with its strong perspectives and fully rounded figures. His use of soft pastel colours contributes to the light atmosphere of the work. PIERO DELLA FRANCESCA was his assistant.

Donatello [Donato di Niccolò] (1386-1468) Florentine sculptor, who trained with GHIBERTI and became the leading figure of the early RENAISSANCE. An early commission for a series of statues for Florence Cathedral (1408-15) and the Or San Michele (1411-13) includes the *St Mark*, the seated *St John the Evangelist* and the famous *St George*, which surmounts a relief demonstrating the technique of *stiacciato*, a method of low-relief drawing in marble, which Donatello brought to prominence. His most classical work is the bronze *David* (1430s), but his reaction against classical principles is evident in later works, e.g. *St John the Baptist* (1457), *Judith and Holofernes* (1456-60) and *St Mary Magdalen* (1465), which are powerful in their emotional intensity.

Dongen, Kees van [Cornelius Theodorus Marie] (1877-1968) Dutch painter, he settled in Paris in 1897 and his early infuences include MONET and IMPRESSIONIST art. His landscapes of the early 1900s are Impressionist in approach, but towards the end of the decade he had introduced a bolder technique in the bright impasto of the FAUVIST style. From 1910 he painted mainly nudes and society portraits, e.g. *Women on the Balcony* (1910).

Doré, Gustave (1832-83) French sculptor, painter and illustrator. He worked originally as a caricaturist for *Le Journal Pour Rire* and became well known for his illustrations of such works as Dante's *Inferno* (1861) and Cervantes' *Don Quixote* (1862). His realistic drawings of London's slums (1872) were used in a government report. His most notable sculpture is the memorial to Alexandre Dumas (1883). Doré's work was admired by van GOGH and the SURREALISTS.

Dou, Gerrit (1613-75) Dutch painter who studied with REMBRANDT, on some of whose works he may have collaborated, e.g. *The Blind Tobit and his Wife Anne* (*c*.1630). Dou's later works are on a small scale, smoothly and precisely painted: he sometimes used a magnifying glass for the fine detail of his carefully composed interiors.

Dove, Arthur Garfield (1880-1946) American painter who studied in Paris, returing to the US in 1910. There he made his living with commercial illustration work while developing his own ABSTRACT painting style based on organic forms, e.g. *Nature Symbolized No. 2* (1914). The development of his style is comparable with the abstract art of his contemporary KANDINSKY. His later work concentrates less on abstract forms and more on the interrelation of areas of colour, as in *High Noon* (1944).

Dubuffet, Jean (1901-85) French painter who studied in
Paris in 1918 but began painting seriously only in 1942.
His work represents a deliberate rejection of established
values in art in favour of a naive style using mixed media. His collection of ART BRUT reflected his interest in the
works of primitives, psychotics and children, and his
ideas about pure, untrained art influenced trends in modern ABSTRACT and SURREALIST art.

Duccio di Buonisegna (*fl*.1278-1318) Italian painter, little of whose work is clearly documented apart from his
masterpiece, the *Maestà* (1311) for the Siena Cathedral
altarpiece. Other works have been attributed to him by
comparison with the *Maestà*, including the *Rucellai Madonna* (1285) in the Uffizzi in Florence and the small
Madonna of the Franciscans (1290). The liveliness and
movement in Duccio's work represents a move away
from Byzantine traditions towards Gothic expressiveness and can be compared with the direction of the work
of GIOTTO in Florence.

Duchamp, Marcel (1887-1968) French-American artist,
founder of the SECTION D'OR group and a prominent figure in American DADA. His early work was influenced by
CUBISM, and his *Nude Descending a Staircase No.2*
(1912) represents a move away from this towards an interest in movement that prefigures FUTURIST trends. He
achieved notoriety in the US with "ready-mades," such
as *Bicycle Wheel* (1913) and with the submission, which
was rejected, to the Society of Independent Artists Exhi-

bition of a urinal under the title *Fountain* (1917). *Large Glass: The Bride Stripped Bare by her Bachelors, Even* (1915-23), although uncompleted, is considered to be his masterpiece.

Duchamp-Villon, Raymond (1876-1918) French sculptor. The brother of Marcel DUCHAMP and Jacques VILLON, he was an important member of the SECTION D'OR group. His earliest work is expressively naturalistic, but from 1910 he became a prominent CUBIST sculptor. His sculptures, based on the human figure, concentrated on masses rather than details. His most famous masterpiece is *The Horse* (1912-14). His promising career was cut short by his death from typhoid at the end of World War I.

Dufy, Raoul (1877-1953) French painter and designer. His early work followed the trends of IMPRESSIONISM, FAUVISM and CUBISM before he developed his own witty, idiosyncratic style during the 1920s. His preferred subjects were racing and boating scenes and the life and high society of the Riviera, painted in bright lively colours and dextrous lines. Notable works include *Riders in the Wood* (1931) and *L'Histoire de l'Electricité* (1938).

Durand, Asher Brown (1796-1886) American painter. He trained first as an engraver, and his early portrait and landscape prints established his reputation in this field. From the 1830s he painted detailed landscapes after the tradition of the HUDSON RIVER SCHOOL. He was a founder, and later a president, of the National Academy of Design. Notable works include *Kindred Spirits* (1849).

Dürer, Albrecht (1471-1528) German engraver and painter. A leading figure of the Northern RENAISSANCE, his work is outstanding in its attention to detail and its emotional content, heightened by his masterly development of a wide range of tonal gradations and textures, e.g. *Melancholia I* (1514). In painting, his influences included the Italian masters, such as Giovanni BELLINI, as in *The Festival of the Rose Gardens* (1506). Later paintings illustrate his sympathies with the Lutheran Reformation, e.g. *Four Apostles* (1526). The scope and variety of his work, both theoretical and practical, was unrivalled in Northern Europe, and his albums of engravings exerted a tremendous influence on North European art.

Dyck, Sir Anthony van (1599-1641) Flemish painter. His early painting was partly influenced by Rubens, in whose studio he worked, but following a period spent in Genoa from 1621 to 1628 he developed his own unique and influential style of portraiture, investing his sitters with extraordinary character and refinement of detail. After 1632, he was court painter to Charles I of England, and his portraits of the nobility influenced court painting and portraiture for the next two hundred years. Most of his English works remain in the Royal Collection, including two portraits of Charles (*c*.1638). Another notable work is *Iconography*, an album of etchings of famous contemporaries, which was completed after his death with reference to his oil sketches and drawings.

E

Eakins, Thomas (1844-1916) American painter. He studied in Paris and was greatly influenced by the works of VELAZQUEZ and RIBERA, which he saw in Madrid. His own work is strongly realistic, as in *The Gross Clinic* (1875), although his portraits show a more dramatic interest in the use of tonal contrasts, reminiscent of REMBRANDT'S work; e.g. *Max Schmitt in a Single Scull* (1871). He was a revolutionary and influential teacher at the Pennsylvania Royal Academy from 1876-86. Other notable works include *The Writing Master* (1881), a portrait of his father, and *The Biglen Brothers Racing* (1873).

Eardley, Joan (1921-63) English-born Scottish painter. She studied at Glasgow School of Art before moving to Catterline on the northeast coast of Scotland, where she spent the rest of her life. Her best-known works are landscapes and seascapes around this area, freely and boldly executed and conveying the power of the sea and the elements. Her sketches and portraits of the Samson children of Glasgow are sensitive, touching and often amusing.

Earl, Ralph (1751-1801) American painter, who studied in London with Benjamin WEST, but was largely uninfluenced in his own strictly realist style. The bulk of his works are portraits of members of wealthy Connecticut families, e.g. *Oliver Ellsworth and his Wife* (1782).

Eight, The A group of American painters comprising GLACKENS, HENRI, LUKS, SLOAN, DAVIES, and others. For the most part they were realist painters and campaigned vigorously on the development of progressive art away from the strictures of academic tradition. Only one exhibition of their work was held, at the Macbeth Galleries in New York in 1908. *See also* ASHCAN SCHOOL.

Eilshemius, Louis Michel (1864-1941) American painter. His earliest works were IMPRESSIONIST-style landscapes, but he later developed a more primitivist approach, e.g. *New York at Night* (1917). He had a one-man show at the Société Anonyme in 1920, but his work subsequently went out of fashion and was restored to popularity only in the 1930s.

El Greco [Domenikos Theotocopoulos] (1541-1614) Cretan-born Spanish painter, sculptor and architect. He studied in Italy, where he was possibly a pupil of TITIAN, although TINTORETTO and MICHELANGELO undoubtedly influenced his work. From 1577 he lived and worked in Toledo. In the main he painted religious subjects, including many portrayals of St Francis. His style was emotional and spiritually evocative, and his palette idiosyncratic in its predominating cold blues and greys at a time when the vogue was for warmer colours. Notable works include *The Burial of Count Orgaz* (1586) and *The Assumption* (1613).

Elsheimer, Adam (1578-1610) German painter and etcher. His early work is in the Flemish Realist tradition, but Italian art influenced the lyricism of his later landscapes and genre paintings. He often combined engraving and painting on copper, working on a small scale, and his attitude is simple and direct, in contrast with the MANNERIST fashion of the time. Notable works include *Rest on the Flight into Egypt* (1609), and he had an important influence on other artists, including RUBENS and REMBRANDT.

engraving A technique of cutting an image into a metal or wood plate using special tools. When ink is applied to the plate, the raised parts will print black and the engraved parts white. The term is also used for a print produced in this way.

Ensor, James (1860-1949) Belgian painter from Ostend. His early work was Impressionistic in the Belgian style, but he gradually lightened his palette and began using a bizarre and fantastic symbolism. His work was exhibited through his membership of Les VINGT, but the strongly expressionistic *Tribulation of St Anthony* (1877) and *Entry of Christ into Brussels* (1888) caused his work to be rejected even by them, and he subsequently gave up painting. The importance of his work was later recognized, and he is considered as a forerunner of EXPRESSIONISM and SURREALISM.

Epstein, Sir Jacob (1880-1959) American-born British sculptor in the Romantic tradition. A great part of his

work aroused controversy in public opinion because of
its alleged indecency, e.g. *The Monument to Oscar Wilde*
(1912) in Paris. His portrait busts, conversely, were
much admired. Important influences on his style include
Wyndham Lewis and some of the Cubist artists. Notable
works include *Christ* (1919), *Genesis* (1931), and *Adam*
(1939).

Ernst, Max (1891-1976) German painter and sculptor.
He was self-taught and, with Jean Arp, founded Dada in
1914; Chirico was among his early influences. He produced bizarre and surreal images in lithograph and photomontage, e.g. *The Elephant Celebes* (1921). He was a
founder member of Surrealism with Breton in 1922 and
moved to the US in 1941. Later works, such as *The
Temptation of St Anthony* (1945), reveal the development of a grotesque, twisted imagery.

Escher, Mauritz Corneille (1898-1970) Dutch graphic
artist famous for his popular optical-illusion drawings,
such as *Endless Staircase*, which persuade the viewer to
see and accept a totally illogical image, or to see one image "hidden" in another.

Estes, Richard (1936-) American painter. His work depicts American streets in a "superrealist" style, revealing
an interest in juxtaposed photographic images and the
interrelation of objects seen behind glass or reflected in
it, e.g. *Foodshop* (1967).

etching A technique of making an engraving in a metal
plate, using acid to bite out·the image rather than tools.

Tones of black or grey can be produced, depending on the extent the acid is allowed to bite. The term is also used for a print produced in this way.

Etty, William (1787-1849) American born English painter, notable mainly for his nude female paintings, which, despite having attracted criticism for weakness in draughtsmanship, display a fine sense of sensual form, texture and colour. He also produced large, complex compositions, such as *The Combat* (1825). Other important works include *Ulysses and the Sirens* (1873) and the *Joan of Arc* triptych (1847).

Evergood, Philip (1901-75) American painter. His early works are of Biblical or genre scenes, but from the 1930s he developed a unique linear style with vibrant colour, consisting of awkwardly drawn figures in a shallow perspective. His preferred subject matter was social-realist issues, e.g. *Lily and the Sparrows*.

Expressionism A term derived from the character of some 20th-century Northern European art, which was coined in a description of an exhibition of Fauvist and Cubist paintings at the Berlin SEZESSION in 1911, but quickly came to be applied to the works of Die BRÜCKE and Der BLAUE REITER. Expressionist works represented a move away from the observational detachment of realism and, to an extent, Impressionist trends, and were concerned with conveying the artist's feelings and emotions as aroused by his subject. Any painting technique that helped to express these feelings was considered a valid medium and included bold, free brushwork, distorted or stylized forms, and vibrant, often violently clashing, colours. The term *expressionist* also refers to an expressive quality of distortion or heightened colour in art from any period or place. *See also* ABSTRACT EXPRESSIONISM.

Eyck, Jan van (d.1441) Dutch painter. Little is known of his early career, but he was court painter to Philip, Duke of Burgundy, from 1425 to about 1430, and all his dated works are from the 1430s, when he lived in Bruges. He was a master in the medium of oil painting, and his representation of light and detail remains unsurpassed. His paintings, while strongly realistic, are imbued with a serene, spiritual atmosphere, as in the famous *Arnolfini Marriage* (1434). Other notable works include the Ghent altarpiece (completed 1432) and *The Man in the Red Turban* (1433).

F

Fabriano, Gentile da *see* **Gentile da Fabriano**.

Fabritius, Carel (1622-54) Dutch painter who studied in REMBRANDT'S studio. His earliest work shows the influence of his master, although he later developed his own style based on a cooler palette. His subject matter included portrait, genre and still lifes as well as animal paintings, of which *Goldfinch* (1654) is a notable example. He was killed in the explosion of the Delft ammunition factory.

Faes, Pieter van der *see* **Lely, Sir Peter**.

Fantin-Latour, Henri (1836-1904) French painter and lithographer. He is best known for his paintings of flowers and his group portraits, such as *Homage to Delacroix* (1864). He also did imaginative lithographic illustrations inspired by the works of Romantic composers like Wagner.

Fauvists a group of French painters including MATISSE, DERAIN, VLAMINCK and others, who painted in a particularly vivid and colourful style. The term *fauve* ("wild animal") was coined as a form of derogatory criticism of an exhibition held at the Salon d'Automne of 1905. Their use of strong, bright colours to express their response to the fierce light of the Mediterranean coast owes something to the influence of GAUGUIN and van GOGH, but they were less interested in representing what they saw and more concerned to express their own feelings in the boldness and freedom of their compositions. Other artists whose work included a Fauvist period were van DONGEN, and DUFY. Although Matisse continued to explore Fauvist techniques, the other artists soon diverged, and the movement as such was fairly short-lived. It was, however, influential in CUBIST and EXPRESSIONIST art.

Federal Arts Project A series of American government aid schemes to assist artists during the years of the Depression, 1933-43. Initially they sponsored civic work on public buildings, but were augmented in 1935 to include a wide range of talents and projects. Most of the US's contemporary major artists of the time were involved in the schemes.

Feininger, Lyonel (1871-1956) American painter. He was in Europe 1887-1937, and worked as a cartoonist before taking up serious painting in 1911. He was involved with the BLAUE REITER. From 1919-33 he taught at the BAUHAUS. His work incorporates CUBIST and FUTURIST features, e.g. *Raddampfer II* (1913), although later pieces, such as *Deep, Sonnenuntergang* (1930) are cooler and more CONSTRUCTIVIST in approach. He often achieved a delightful sense of EXPRESSIONIST fantasy reminiscent of his early satirical drawings.

Fergusson, John Duncan (1874-1961) Scottish painter, one of the Scottish COLOURISTS. His earliest works show the influences of WHISTLER and the GLASGOW SCHOOL. Later work, dating from a period spent in Paris, (1907-14) is more FAUVIST, as in the bold use of colour and free brushwork of *Rogan Harbour, Evening*, or the dynamics of his group paintings, e.g. *Rhythm* (1911). An important collection of his work was gifted to Stirling University.

figurative art or representational art Art that recognizably represents figures, objects or animals from real life, as opposed to ABSTRACT ART.

Filipepi, Alessandro di Mariano *see* **Botticelli, Sandro**.

fine arts *see* **applied arts**.

Flaxman, John (1755-1826) English sculptor and designer. He studied at the Royal Academy in London and worked for Josiah Wedgewood, where his low-relief design and portraits developed his strong sense of line and detail. He was also a proficient illustrator, and his work on the *Iliad* and the *Odyssey* (1793) influenced continental artists, such as INGRES. From 1810 he occupied the newly created chair of sculpture at the Royal Academy. Important monuments include those of the Earl of Mansfield (1801) at Westminster Cathedral, Nelson (1810) at St Paul's, and the delicate relief of Agnes Cromwell (1800) at Chichester.

Flemalle, Master of *see* **Campin, Robert**.

Forain, Jean Louis (1852-1931) French painter and caricaturist. He made his living with the Paris journals, *Le*

Scapin and *La Vie Parisienne,* and was influenced in his early paintings by REMBRANDT and GOYA. His work reveals the cartoonist's economical sense of line and gesture. He exhibited with the Impressionists, although he used a less colourful palette, and his main influences were MANET and DEGAS. Notable works include *The Tribunal* (1884), and *Counsel and Accused* (1908).

Fouquet, Jean (*c*.1420-1481) French painter. Little of his work is documented, and while he is known to have travelled in Italy and to have painted a portrait, since lost, of Pope Eugenius IV, his style was largely uninfluenced by Italian art. His early patrons include Etienne Chevalier, who commissioned his *Book of Hours* (1460) and the Melun diptych, *Madonna and Child* (*c*.1450). He was also court painter to Louis XI from 1475. His work is dominated by his excellent draughtsmanship, bringing a grace and purity to miniatures and larger works alike, as in Josephus' *Jewish Antiquities* (1470-76).

found object *or* **objet trouvé** A form of art that began with DADA and continued with SURREALISM, where an object, either natural or manufactured, is displayed as a piece of art in its own right.

Fragonard, Jean-Honoré (1732-1806) French painter. One of the greatest exponents of ROCOCO, he studied with CHARDIN and BOUCHER. His early works were historical scenes on a grand scale, e.g. *Coreseus Sacrificing himself to Save Callierhoe* (1765), but he is best known for his smaller, picturesquely pretty canvases, such as

The Swing (1766). His patrons included Madame de Pompadour and Madame du Barry, for whom he painted the four *Progress of Love* paintings (1771-3). His frivolous style went out of vogue during the French Revolution, and he died in poverty.

Francesca, Piero della *see* **Piero della Francesca**.

Francis, Sam (1923-) American painter. He studied in California and Paris, where he met RIOPELLE and was influenced by ART INFORMEL painters. Other influences included Japanese art and American abstract expressionists, such as Jackson POLLOCK, e.g. *Big Red* (1953). His first one-man show was in 1952 in Paris, and he had several retrospective exhibitions during the 1960s.

Frankenthaler, Helen (1928-) American painter. Her early influences included GORKY and POLLOCK, and her work forms a significant link between ABSTRACT EXPRESSIONISM and COLOUR FIELD PAINTING. From Pollock she learned a canvas-staining technique, which she developed with the use of strong acrylic colours to create a complete synthesis of colour and surface. Notable works include *Mountains and Sea* (1952).

French, Daniel Chester (1850-1931) American sculptor, best known for his civic commissions. These include *The Minute Man* (1875) in Concord, Massachusetts, and the seated figure of *Abraham Lincoln* (1922) in Washington DC.

fresco A painting directly painted on to a wall that has previously been covered with a damp freshly laid layer of lime plaster, the paint and plaster reacting chemically to become stable and permanent. Fresco painting worked particularly well in the warm, dry climate of Italy, where it reached its peak in the 16th century.

Freud, Lucien (1922-) German-born British artist, who settled in England in 1931. His expressive linear style is evident in *Girl with Roses* (1947-8) and has been described as "hyper-realist." Later works display a more painterly style and freer brushwork, without, however, losing their hypnotic intensity, e.g. *Francis Bacon* (1952).

Friedrich, Caspar David (1774-1840) German Romantic painter, who studied at Copenhagen and settled in Dresden in 1798. He was largely uninfluenced by other artists or trends, and his work was highly controversial due to his treatment of landscape, e.g. *The Cross on the Mountain* (1808). His works have a melancholy atmosphere peculiar to the Northern European temperament: land, sea and sky are fused in strange crepuscular light or hazy mist, out of which emerge trees and ruins. The strong sense of emotion and spiritual feeling in his work was an important development in landscape painting, although Friedrich himself died in poverty and his significance was recognized only towards the end of the 19th century.

Fry, Roger *see* **Post-Impressionism**

Fuseli, Henry (1741-1825) Swiss painter. He originally trained for the priesthood but took up painting and settled in England in 1765. He was much influenced by the great painters of the Italian RENAISSANCE, particularly MICHELANGELO, and his paintings are mannered and romantic with a strange sense of the grotesque and macabre, which was later to appeal to SURREALIST artists. He was professor of painting at the Royal Academy in London, where ETTY, LANDSEER and CONSTABLE were among his pupils. Notable works include *The Nightmare* (1872) and *The Witches in Macbeth*.

Futurism a movement of artists and writers formed by the poet Filippo Marinetti (1876-1944) in Italy in 1909. BOCCIONI and CARRÀ were among the painters in the group, whose aim was to convey a sense of movement and dynamism, as in Boccioni's *The City Rises* (1910). As a group, the Futurists published manifestos on various aspects of the arts, and exhibitions toured Europe during 1911-12. The original group had broken up by the end of World War I, but their work and ideas had a resounding influence on subsequent art movements.

G

Gabo Naum [Naum Neemia Pevsner] (1890-1979) Russian-born sculptor, he initially studied medicine and engineering but took up sculpture in 1916. His early works were based on a kind of geometric CUBISM which came to be seen as the origins of CONSTRUCTIVISM. He was one of the first to experiment with KINETIC ART and to make use of lightweight and transparent modern materials to enhance the delicate balance and sense of weightlessness of his work. In Russia, together with his brother Antoine PEVSNER, he published their *Realistic Manifesto* (1920), which set out the principles of Constructivism. It represents a turning away from the style of TATLIN and MALEVICH, whose work they found too utilitarian in approach. In 1922 Gabo moved to Berlin and exhibited there, in Paris (1924) and in the US (1926) with van DOESBURG and Pevsner. He had a one-man show in 1938 at the London Gallery before settling in the US, where he taught at Harvard and was elected to the Institute of American Academy of Arts and Letters. Important commissions include sculptures for the Baltimore Museum of Art (1951) and a relief for the United States Rubber Company in the Rockefeller Center, New York (1956).

Gainsborough, Thomas (1727-88) English painter, his earliest influences were WATTEAU and the ROCOCO painters. Mature works such as *The Blue Boy* (1770) show some influence of RUBENS and van DYCK, but essentially Gainsborough's own individual style is predominant. He worked as a portrait painter, first in his native Suffolk and later in Bath, before moving to London in 1774 where he was a founder member of the Royal Academy. His keen interest in landscape painting pervades most of his work, his sitters often being portrayed in an outdoor setting, e.g *Mr and Mrs Andrews* (1748). He developed a light, rapid painting style based on a delicate palette and at all times demonstrating his own delight in painting. Later works include his "fancy" paintings or imaginary landscapes and portraits, e.g. *Peasant Girl Gathering Sticks* (1782). Other major masterpieces include *Mary, Countess Howe* (1774), *The Cottage Door* (1780) and *The Watering Place* (1777).

Gauguin, Paul (1848-1903) French painter, printmaker and sculptor, one of the greatest exponents of POST-IMPRESSIONISM. He was brought up in Peru and worked as a stockbroker before taking up painting in 1873. He exhibited in three IMPRESSIONIST exhibitions before he began to develop his own simplistic, richly coloured style. *The Vision after the Sermon*, or *Jacob wrestling with the Angel* (1888), inspired by the lifestyle of Breton peasants at Pont-Aven, marks the beginning of this development. During his Breton period he exerted a powerful influence on other artists, in particular the NABIS and the SYMBOLISTS, and this influence has also extended into 20th-century EXPRESSIONIST painting. Gauguin's interest in primitive and simplistic art led him to make his home in the South Pacific Islands where, despite illness and poverty, he painted some of his most important masterpieces, including *Where do we come from? What are we? Where are we going?* (1897)

genre The French word for "type" or "sort," used to denote a category of painting, e.g. landscape, still life, etc.

genre painting A painting that has as its subject a scene from everyday life, as opposed to a historical event, mythological scene, etc. Genre paintings appear in the backgrounds of Medieval paintings, but it was the Dutch painters, e.g. BRUEGEL, BOSCH and VERMEER, who were the first to specialize in them and to continue the tradition. In France, CHARDIN used genre scenes to great effect, but they did not become really popular with painters until the Realists, e.g. COURBET and MILLET. British painters, e.g. HOGARTH, GAINSBOROUGH and WILKIE, painted genre scenes, but gradually the distinction between such scenes and other genres of painting has blurred.

Gentile da Fabriano (*c.*1370-1427) Italian painter in the INTERNATIONAL GOTHIC tradition. Little of his work has survived, but he is thought to have established his reputation with frescos, since lost, for the Doge's Palace in Venice. He was held in high regard in Siena, Florence and Rome. His best-known surviving masterpiece is the *Adoration of the Magi* (1423), now in the Ufizzi in Florence. He was a contemporary of GHIBERTI and exerted a great influence on younger artists: PISANELLO, BELLINI and Fra ANGELICO were among his pupils and followers.

Gentileschi, Orazio (1563-1639) Italian painter, his earliest work was MANNERIST in style but the major influence on his art was his friend and older contemporary CARAVAGGIO. His paintings were poetic and clearly drawn, as in the graceful *Annunciation* (*c.*1623). He moved to England in 1626, where he was commissioned by Charles I to paint the ceilings of the Queen's house. His work at this time was less Caravaggesque in style and lighter in colour and mood. His daughter **Artemisia Gentileschi** (1593-*c.*1652), however, was a powerful exponent of the Caravaggesque style and was responsible for its predominance in Naples, where she settled in 1630. Her earliest known masterpiece is *Susannah and the Elders* (1610) and a favourite theme was *Judith and Holofernes*, which she represented in several paintings.

Géricault, Théodore (1791-1824) French painter. He studied in the classical tradition and his early work was influenced by RUBENS, but his mature style took its direction from his admiration of the works of MICHELANGELO. The realism and baroque dynamism of *The Raft of the Medusa* (1819) caused nearly as much outrage as its political overtones, and his powerful, direct oil sketches, such as *The Derby at Epsom* (1820), exerted a huge influence on younger painters. Géricault is seen as the originator of ROMANTICISM in painting.

Ghiberti, Lorenzo (1378-1455) Florentine sculptor. The span of his work covers the late Gothic and early Renaissance periods, of which times he was an outstanding and and highly talented figure. His masterpieces are the two sets of gilded bronze doors for the Baptistry in Florence. He worked on these from 1401 to 1452, giving training and employment to most of the major contemporary artists in his workshops. The difference of approach between the two pairs of doors aptly illustrates Ghiberti's early Gothic style and the later predominance of Renaissance principles. Other important works include life-size bronzes of *St John the Baptist* (1412-16); *St Matthew* (1419) and *St Stephen* (1425-29). He also wrote two *Commentaries*, one a history of Italian art and the other an autobiography. DONATELLO, UCCELLO and MASOLINO were among his pupils.

Ghirlandaio, Domenico (1449-94) Florentine painter, who ran a workshop, together with his brothers **Benedetto** (1458-97) and **Davide** (1452-1525), where he produced frescos and altarpieces for a number of churches in Florence, e.g. *The Life of St John the Baptist* (1845-90) in the Church of Santa Maria Novella, as well as in San Gimigniano and in the Sistine Chapel in Rome: *The Calling of the Apostles* (1481-2). He was also a portraitist of some stature and his tempera studies are detailed and compassionate, as in *The Old Man and his*

Grandson. An interesting feature of his major works is his use of contemporary portraits in his frescos. His son **Ridolfo** (1483-1561) was also a portrait painter, and MICHELANGELO was his pupil.

Giacometti, Alberto (1901-66) Swiss painter and sculptor. He studied in Paris, experimenting in CUBISM and CONSTRUCTIVISM, and was a member of the SURREALISTS from 1930-35. From this period his highly individual style developed and was finally widely recognized after a major exhibition in New York in 1948. Representative works include *Four_Women on a Base* (1950), *Café* (1931) and *The Cage (Woman and Head)* (1950). Throughout his career he struggled with the problems of representing more than the the visual reality of his subject, particularly in portraiture. In sculpture he was also concerned with space and perspective in relation to the scale of his figure groups. While Giacometti's work is thoroughly unique and individual, he is perhaps best described as an existentialist artist.

Giambologna *see* **Bologna, Giovanni.**

Giorgione del Castelfranco (1475-1510) Venetian painter. Virtually none of his work is accurately documented and little has survived, but he is accepted as having been one of the most influential painters of his time. He is thought to have studied with BELLINI, and was a contemporary of TITIAN. He painted the *Castelfranco Altarpiece* in his native town, and other works, authenticated by surviving fragments or engravings or by the

writings of Marcantonio Michiel and VASARI, include
paintings for the Doge's Palace (1507-9) and frescos for
the Fondaco dei Tedeschi in Venice (1508). The bulk of
Giorgione's work was in small private commissions,
typical of which are *The Tempest* and *The Three Philosophers*. *The Concert Chapitre* may have been painted by
Giorgione or Titian. The critical importance of his work
is in his treatment of landscape; he was one of the first to
imbue landscape painting with strong atmospheres and
moods to which the detail is subordinated, and in this he
was much admired and imitated by younger and succeeding generations of Venetian painters.

Giotto di Bondone (1267-1337) Florentine painter and
architect. Little of his work is documented, but his
known and accredited works show a development of
spatial perspective and fully rounded figures that represent a departure from the flat, decorative imagery of the
Byzantine era. The most important works accepted as his
are the frescos of *The Life of the Virgin, St Anne and St
Joachim* and *The Life and Passion of Christ* (1313) in
the Arena Chapel in Padua, but great controversy sur-
rounds the attribution of *The Life of St Francis* frescos in
the Church of San Francesco at Assisi (*c.*1290s). Among
the many panel paintings thought to be by Giotto is the
Ognissanti Madonna (*c.*1308) in the Ufizzi, Florence.
Giotto exerted an enormous influence over the next generation of Florentine painters, and his work is now taken
to represent the starting point of modern western art.

Giovanni Bologna *see* **Bologna, Giovanni.**

Giulio Romano *see* **Raphael.**

Glackens, William James (1870-1938) American painter. He studied at the Pennsylvania Academy of the Fine Arts and was influenced and encouraged as a serious artist by his friend Robert HENRI, whom he met in 1891, although he continued to earn his living by art journalism and illustration. He was a member of the New York Realists and The EIGHT, and a leading figure of the ASHCAN SCHOOL, although his work has a strong Impressionist style, as in *Chez Mouqin* (1905). He was involved in organizing the ARMORY SHOW, in which he exhibited, and a memorial exhibition of his own work was held at the Whitney Museum of American Art in 1938.

Glasgow Boys *or* **Glasgow School** A group of painters centred in Glasgow in the 1880s and 90s. They represented a move away from academic strictures and were inspired by the *plein air* BARBIZON SCHOOL. They established an outpost of the European vogue for naturalism and romantic lyricism in landscape painting, and their influence extends into the 20th century, particularly in Scottish landscape painting. Members of the group included LAVERY, HENRY, HORNEL and GUTHRIE.

Goes, Hugo van der (*d*.1482) Flemish painter from Ghent, where he joined the painters' guild in 1467 and became dean in 1475 before entering a Brussels monastery. His major work, on which attribution of others is based, is the Medici commission for the *Portinari Altarpiece* (1746), now in the Uffizzi in Florence, which shows a rich sense of decorative surface texture combined with outstanding perception of space and depth of composition. The subject is the *Adoration of the Child*, and the landscape of the centre panel extends to the wings, where the saints and the patron's family are depicted. Other important works include *The Adoration of the Magi* (1470) and *The Death of the Virgin* (1480).

Gogh, Vincent van (1853-90) Dutch painter. He originally studied theology and was a lay preacher before taking up painting in 1880. He studied at the Antwerp Academy, but his work remained thoroughly unacademic in its realist subject matter and bold, expressionistic style, e.g. *The Potato Eaters* (1885). He moved to Paris in 1886 where his work was variously influenced by DEGAS, GAUGUIN and SEURAT, although without compromising his enigmatic use of colour and powerful impasto brushwork. He spent the last two years of his life in the south of France, partly in an asylum at St Rémy; it was a time of intense creativity arising out of personal anguish, e.g. *The Cornfield* (1889). His importance in the establishment of a new direction to EXPRESSIONIST and ABSTRACT ART is enormous, and his work had a resonant and continuing influence on 20th-century art worldwide.

Gorky, Arshile [Vosdanig Manoog Adoian] (1905-48) Armenian-born American painter who studied and taught at the Grand Central School of Art in New York.

His early work shows the influence of his friend DE KOONING and of CUBIST art, as in T*he Artist and his Mother* (1926-9). He worked on the FEDERAL ARTS PROJECT in the 1930s, painting an abstract mural, now destroyed, for Newark Airport. In the 1940s he began to establish his own bright, free-flowing style from the assimilation of Cubist and more organic abstract forms, typified by a series of paintings of *Garden in Sochi* (1941) and *The Liver is the Cock's Comb* (1944). Gorky's later works are more subdued in colour range following a series of personal crises and disasters, and he committed suicide.

Gossaert, Jan, called **Mabuse** (*c.*1478-1533) Flemish painter from Mabeuge, he was a master of the Antwerp Guild and Philip of Burgundy was his patron. His early work shows the influence of van EYCK and van der GOES, but he later included elements of Italian art, and his work is a curious yet dignified admixture of Flemish portraits and figures in classical poses, as in *St Luke* (1515) and *Danaë* (1527). He undertook several royal commissions, for which he travelled widely, and he had a notable influence on European art. Major works include *Adoration of the Magi* (1507-8).

Gothic A style of architecture that lasted from the 12th to the 16th centuries in Northern Europe and Spain. Its effect on art was to produce the INTERNATIONAL GOTHIC style.

gouache An opaque mixture of watercolour paint and

white pigment, which is also called **poster paint** *or* **body paint**.

Goujon, Jean (*c.*1510-68) French sculptor, who was responsible for developing a sculptural parallel to the MANNERIST traditions then in vogue in writing and painting. Nothing is known of his early life and works, although it seems likely that he travelled in Italy and had a knowledge of Italian architecture and sculpture. He was also looked on as an authority on the ANTIQUE. Notable works include the pillars in the Church of St Maclou near Rouen, and the caryatids at the Louvre in Paris. Goujon fled France as a Protestant exile after 1562, and is thought to have died in Bologna.

Goya y Lucientes, Francisco de (1746-1828) Spanish painter and printmaker, who studied in Madrid, where he finally settled in 1775. Early works contain elements of NEOCLASSICAL and ROCOCO styles, but the major influences on his art were TIEPOLO and VELAZQUÉZ, who inspired his strong, free-flowing technique and powerful pictorial style. Early pieces include frescos for the Church of San Antonio da Florida and portraits of the royal family, to whom he was court painter from 1786. Important later works include the etchings *Los Caprichos* (1799) and *Disasters of War* (1810-20) and reveal his dislike of the established church and state, as well as his later outrage at the behaviour of an invading French army. The famous paintings of *May 2nd 1808* and *May 3rd 1808* also form a dramatic and moving record of wartime atrocities. His works of later years, known as his "Black Paintings," also demonstrate an abhorrence of human cruelty. Goya spent his last years in exile in France.

Gris, Juan [José Gonzalez] (1887-1927) Spanish painter who studied in Madrid before moving to Paris in 1906. ART NOUVEAU was an early influence on his work prior to meeting PICASSO in 1910. His work in the CUBIST style developed into the more abstract form of Synthetic Cubism, and he was an early experimenter in COLLAGE. Most of his paintings have a constructivist approach, as in *Homage to Picasso* (1912), but later works, such as *Violin and Fruit Dish* (1924), are more freely painted. Gris also designed stage sets and costumes for Diaghilev's Ballet Russe.

grisaille A monochrome painting made using only shades of grey, often used as a sketch for oil paintings.

Gropius, Walter *see* **Bauhaus**.

Gros, Antoine Jean (1771-1835) French painter who studied under DAVID and was influenced by RUBENS and the Venetian painters. In 1793 he met Napoleon and became his official war painter, travelling with the armies and recording battle campaigns in a bold and vivid manner that won him great acclaim. He is seen as a forerunner of the ROMANTIC movement in France, although he later tried to revert to his early classical training, the lack of success of which lead to his suicide in 1835. Notable works include *The Plague at Jaffa* (1804) and *The Battle* *of Aboukir* (1806). He also decorated the cupola of the Pantheon in Paris. BONINGTON, DELACROIX and GÉRICAULT were all pupils of Gros.

Grosz, George (1893-1959) German painter, cartoonist and illustrator. He was a prominent member of DADA and established his early reputation with caricatures for the satirical press. Important collections of his work, such as *The Face of the Ruling Class* (1821) and *Ecce Homo* (1927), represent his fiercely anti-fascist and anti-capitalist views. He settled in the US in the 1930s and taught at the Art Students' League, New York. Later paintings are more mellow and less political in approach, as in a number of café and street scenes, e.g. N*ew York Harbour* (1936), although some works are still surreal and terrifying, e.g. *The Pit* (1946). Grosz has been hailed by critics as a satirist ranking alongside DAUMIER, GOYA and HOGARTH.

grotesque A term for a style of ornamentation that began in Roman times and reached its height with ROCOCO. It consisted of a series of figurative or floral ornaments in decorative frames that are linked by festoons.

Grünewald, Matthias [Mathis Godhardt-Niethardt] (*c*.1460-1528) German painter, whose few surviving works include religious paintings and altarpieces, most important of which is the altarpiece commissioned for the monastery at Isenheim (1515), now in the Musée d'Unterlinden, Colmar. His competent use of perspective, gothic imagery, strong colour and an expressionistic style of distortion all combine to produce a powerful and intensely emotional vision of Christ's suffering. He is also known to have produced a number of smaller paintings, although unlike many North European artists of the time, he did little in the way of engraving. He was an influential painter among younger contemporaries such as BALDUNG GRIEN, DÜRER and Hans HOLBEIN the Younger.

Guardi, Francesco (1712-93) Venetian painter. He is known mainly for his views of Venice, painted in a free, expressive style in contrast to the detailed compositions of his older contemporary CANALETTO. Guardi was a prolific artist, painting historical and religious subjects, still lifes and imaginary views, but his patrons and agents were not significant enough to raise him out of the obscurity and poverty in which he eventually died. His brother **Giovanni Antonio** (1699-1760) ran the family studio, and it is uncertain which of the brothers painted the outstanding *Story of Tobit* (*c*.1755) in the Church of San Raffaele.

Guercino, Il [Giovanni Francesco Barbieri] (1591-1666) Italian BAROQUE painter from Centro. His early influences include the Venetian painters and Ludovico CARRACCI, and his works are distinguished by their dramatic sense of light and colour, soft, well-rounded forms and excellent draughtsmanship. His best-known work is the *Aurora* ceiling fresco (1621-3) in the Villa Ludovisi in Rome, where he lived at that time. He later settled in

Bologna, where his mature work took on a more classical aspect although remaining painterly in style, and his career was long and successful.

Guston, Philip (1913-80) American painter. His early figurative works are concerned with social issues, and he worked on murals for the WPA (the Works Progress Administration), set up under the FEDERAL ARTS PROJECT. Later works are more abstract and lyrical, concerned with the interaction of colours, and his mature work includes pieces of a more sinister atmosphere, notably his series on the Klu Klux Klan.

Guthrie, Sir James (1859-1930) Scottish painter and member of the GLASGOW SCHOOL. He spent much of his time in the village of Cockburnspath, inspired by the *plein air* painting of the BARBIZON SCHOOL. He later moved to Glasgow, where he enjoyed a successful career in portrait painting. His works are subtle in tone and full of realism without sacrificing a good sense of decorative line and colour. Along with the other Glasgow Boys, he has had an influence on younger generations of Scottish painters.

Gwathmey, Robert (1903-　) American painter whose work is linear and colourful in a stylistically simplified style. A common theme is the life of southern black workers, as in *Workers on the Land* (1947).

H

Hals, Frans (*c*.1581-1666) Dutch painter. His early life and works are not well documented, but he is thought to have studied in Haarlem. His first major work is *The Banquet of the St George Civic Guard* (1616), a lively and innovative group portrait and a move away from formal trends in group portraiture. His fresh, natural spontaneity and a sound understanding of the works of Caravaggio combine in the famous *Laughing Cavalier* (1624). His mature works, while still freshly and sensitively composed, are more sombre in colour and mood, e.g. *The Regents* and *The Regentesses of the Almshouse* (both *c.* 1664). Hals had a large family and all his numerous commissions could not keep him out of the poverty in which he eventually died. Several of his sons became painters.

Hamilton, Gavin (1723-98) Scottish painter. He trained in Scotland before settling permanently in Rome from 1775, where he was involved in the Neoclassical circle of Mengs. His influences included the Antique and the works of Poussin, and his history paintings were copied in engravings and were influential among succeeding generations of Neoclassical painters, including David.

Hanson, Duane (1925-) American sculptor famous for his realistically detailed figures modelled out of fibreglass resin, and using real garments and objects as props. The themes of most of these works tend to be American stereotypes of one kind or another, e.g. *Tourists* (1970) represents middle-class lack of taste or self-awareness.

Hare, David (1917-) American sculptor. He originally trained as a photographer and was involved with the Surrealist movement in the 1940s. His best-known pieces are metalwork sculptures, such as *Juggler* (1950), which show his concern with linear and spatial forms.

Hartley, Marsden (1877-1943)   American abstract painter. He travelled to Paris and Berlin from 1912-15, and was associated with Kandinsky. His earlier works are bright and decorative, as in *A German Officer* (1914), but mature pieces include more atmospheric, troubled landscapes dependent on mass and line, e.g. *Lobster Fishermen* (1940-41).

Haydon, Benjamin Robert (1786-1846) English painter, whose talents did not quite match his aspirations to raise the timbre of British history painting to the Grand Manner. He was a Romantic and a friend of the poets Keats and Wordsworth, whose portraits he painted. He is known to have been an eloquent lecturer and writer, passionate in his defence of the arts. His own paintings, however, tended to be awkward and melodramatic. A typical work is *The Maid of Saragossa* . He was thwarted in his ambition to decorate the Houses of Parliament with frescos. He finally developed a paranoia that led to suicide.

Hague School *see* **Mauve, Anton.**

Henri, Robert [Robert Henry Cozad] (1865-1929) American painter who studied at the Pennsylvania Academy of Art and at the Ecole des Beaux Arts in Paris. Early influences included Thomas EAKINS and Frans HALS. He also admired the works of MANET and pioneered the movement to bring art out of the academies to the people in America. He was a leader of The EIGHT and a founder member of the ASHCAN SCHOOL. The major import of his work is the social realism of his subject matter, based on a deeply held belief that artists should paint life around them as they saw it. Typical of his work is *West 57th St., New York* (1902). Some of his best works are portraits, such as *Laughing Child* and *The Masquerade Dress: A Portrait of Mrs Robert Henri* (1911).

Henry, George (1858-1943) Scottish painter and member of the GLASGOW SCHOOL. One of his best-known paintings is *Galloway Landscape* (1889), illustrating a favourite theme of cattle in landscape. His approach is simplistic in style, highlighting a strongly decorative sense of line and colour. He collaborated on two paintings with his friend HORNEL: *The Druids* (1889) and *The Star in the East* (1890). He later settled in London, where he founded the Chelsea Art Club.

Hepworth, Dame Barbara (1903-75) English sculptor. She trained at the Royal College of Art in London, where she was a contemporary of Henry MOORE and of Ben NICHOLSON, to whom she was married (1932-51). Her preference was for direct carving rather than the hitherto favoured techniques of modelling and casting sculptural pieces. An early work, *Figure in Sycamore* (1931), demonstrates her acute sensitivity to the natural appropriateness of the material to the subject in her work. Pierced holes and scooped-out hollows in wood and stone carvings were experiments in depth and perspective that she later developed by painting parts of the hollows and stretching strings over the openings, as in *Pelagos* (1946). Along with Moore, she was one of the most innovative and celebrated British sculptors of the 20th century. After her death in a fire, her studio and garden at St Ives were established as a museum of her work.

history painting A GENRE of painting that takes as its subject a scene from history (particularly ancient history), religious or mythological legend, or from great works of literature, e.g. by Dante or Shakespeare.

Hockney, David (1937-) English artist, whose versatility in the fields of painting, printmaking, photography and design makes it hard to confine him to any one category. His unorthodox artistic development and infinite variety of sources are all underpinned by his outstanding draughtsmanship. Hockney achieved distinction while still a student at the Royal College of Art in London, winning a number of prestigious awards. Public acclaim came with the exhibition in 1963 of a set of 16 etchings entitled *Rake's Progress*. He designed sets and costumes for Jarry's *Ubu Roi* in 1966. His early works are stylistically naive, and here he acknowledges a debt to DUBUFFET, but to classify Hockney as a pop artist is to miss the point of his depth and diversity. Paintings such as *We Two Boys Forever Clinging* (1961) and *Peter getting out of Nick's Pool* (1966) illustrate the recurring themes in his work of homosexuality and a fascination with the reflective surface of water. Hockney has held teaching posts at the universities of Iowa, Colorado and California, where he lives.

Hogarth, William (1697-1764) English artist. He trained first as an engraver in the ROCOCO tradition, and by 1720 had established his own illustration business. He then began his series of paintings known as "conversation pieces," e.g. *A Scene from The Beggar's Opera* (late 1720s) of which there is a version in the Tate Gallery, London. By the 1730s he was also painting some fine portrait commissions in a lively and direct manner e.g. *Captain Coram* (1740). The reason he did not achieve the status of a successful portraitist is that he was not inclined to flatter his sitters. Also about this time he began to produce his series paintings comprising six to eight pictures that followed a sequential narrative in the manner of tableaux in a stage play. They tended to illustrate vice and punishment and to satirize moral values. The best known of these is *Marriage à la Mode* (1742-4). He also wrote a treatise on aesthetic principles entitled *The Analysis of*

Beauty (1753). Hogarth was an influential figure in painting, and his contribution to the development of satiric art is immeasurable.

Holbein, Hans [the Younger] (*c.*1479-1543) German painter. He began his career in Basel, where Erasmus was one of his major patrons. He painted mainly portraits and religious paintings, the most important of which is *The Death of Christ* (1521), memorable and moving in its realism. His portraits were minutely detailed and exactly drawn, as in the painting of *Thomas More as Lord Chancellor* (1527), which he painted on a visit to England. He also painted *Sir Thomas More and his Family* (1527), which is thought to be the first ever domestic group portrait. In Basel he had produced a set of 51 woodcuts entitled *The Dance of Death*, the egalitarian message of which gained popularity with the spread of the Reformed Church. At the same time church patronage declined, and Holbein moved to England where he became court painter to Henry VIII, and painted the full-length portrait that has come to be the representative image of that monarch. He painted numerous royal portraits, but unfortunately many of his original works have been lost or destroyed and are now only represented by original sketches or copies. Holbein was also a great miniaturist and designer, and an outstanding influence on succeeding generations of painters.

Homer, Winslow (1836-1910) American painter. He trained first in lithography and worked as a war illustrator for *Harper's Weekly* during the Civil War. His first paintings owe something to the directness and detachment of early photography, but he was subsequently influenced by the works of MANET. Clear, bright paintings like *Breezing Up* (1876) are typical of his style and show the sea as a favourite theme. He spent 1881-2 in the northeast of England before settling on the coast of Maine in the US, painting powerful oils and watercolours of dramatically stormy seas, e.g. *Northeaster* (1895).

Honthorst, Gerrit van (1590-1656) Dutch painter from Utrecht. He spent the years 1610-20 in Italy and was deeply influenced by the work of CARAVAGGIO, evidenced in the paintings *Christ before the High Priest* (1617) and *Samson and Delilah* (1620). Thereafter he returned to Holland, where he was a prominent figure in the UTRECHT SCHOOL, and over the next decade his tonal range became lighter and less dramatic. From the 1630s he was court painter at The Hague and painted a number of royal portraits there and abroad, including Charles I of England and members of the Danish royal family. While his later career was internationally successful, his early Caravaggesque period was to have more lasting influence on future artists.

Hooch *or* **Hoogh, Pieter de** (*c*.1629-*c*.1684) Dutch painter from Rotterdam, who is thought to have trained in Haarlem. His still, peaceful interior and garden-figure compositions are absolutely typical of Dutch painting of

the time, e.g. *The Courtyard of a House in Delft* (1658).
He was an older contemporary of VERMEER but was probably influenced by the younger artist. His later works are more ambitious but lack the quality of his early pieces, e.g. *A Musical Party* (1675-77).

Hopper, Edward (1882-1976) American painter. He studied at the Chase School of Art with Robert HENRI and was a member of the ASHCAN SCHOOL. His initial influences include MANET and DEGAS. Early etchings and watercolours are concerned with the urban realism that was to dominate his later work. His major paintings have a quiet presence intensified by the use of strong morning and evening light. The heavy stillness of deserted streets and the passive isolation of his figures, as in *Early Sunday Morning* (1930), give rise to feelings of intense sadness.

Hornel, Edward Arthur (1864-1933) Scottish painter and member of the GLASGOW SCHOOL. He collaborated with his friend George HENRY on *The Druids* (1889) and *The Star in the East* (1890) as well as travelling with Henry to Japan. Japanese art further influenced the development of the colourful and linear quality of his work. A favourite theme was children playing in fields of flowers or by streams, usually painted in a rich colourful decorative impasto.

Houdon, Jean-Antoine (1741-1828) French sculptor who studied with PIGALLE and won the Prix de Rome in 1761. In Rome from 1764-8 he achieved initial fame with the figures *L'Ecorche* (1764) and *St Bruno* (1767). He then went on to establish his reputation in portrait busts, examples of which are *Gluck* (1775), *Voltaire* and *Benjamin Franklin* (1778). He was commissioned for a marble statue of *George Washington* (1791) for the Virginia State Capitol in Richmond. Houdon survived the French Revolution but achieved little of note afterwards.

Hudson River School A group of American landscape painters active in the mid-19th century. Leading figures were COLE and DURAND, and their work was concerned with the beauty and mysticism of nature, expressed in romantic terms on a grand and noble scale. They were influenced by the writers Fenimore Cooper and Washington Irving as well as by TURNER.

Hunt, William Holman (1827-1910) English painter and a founder of the PRE-RAPHAELITE movement. Along with his friend MILLAIS, he was opposed to the frivolity of established trends in contemporary art and sought to express the Pre-Raphaelite aims of direct study from nature and natural composition. He is known to have made several journeys to the Middle East to paint accurate detail for his Biblical scenes. He was deeply religious, and his paintings have a strong moralistic message and symbolic attention to detail, as in *The Light of the World* or *The Awakening Conscience* (1854). His work generally lacks grace and sensitivity in its colour and composition, and apart from its strength of conviction, is not now held in particularly high regard.

Hunt, William Morris (1824-79) American painter who studied in Paris and was associated with the BARBIZON SCHOOL. He returned to the US where he promoted the Barbizon artists and exerted considerable influence on his American contemporaries through his own landscape and figure paintings. Much of his work was lost in a fire in 1872, and his only extant works of any note are his murals in the New York State Capitol, Albany. The writer Henry James was his pupil.

Hunter, George Leslie (1877-1931) Scottish painter and member of the group referred to as the Scottish COLOURISTS. He was influenced by FAUVIST painting, and his delight in the richnesses and relationships of colour is evident in most of his work. A typical example is *Reflections, Balloch*. Landscapes and still lifes with fruit or flowers were common themes.

I

Ibbetson, Julius Caesar (1759-1817) English painter who established himself in London copying other works for dealers and imitating the Dutch landscape painters and GAINSBOROUGH. From 1800 he settled in his native Yorkshire, where he painted landscapes and coastal scenes with figures. His work is essentially English and picturesque in style. He also painted some portraits, typical of which is one of the poet Robert Burns in a Scottish landscape setting.

icon *or* **ikon** A religious image, usually painted on a wooden panel, regarded as sacred in the Byzantine Church and subsequently by the Orthodox Churches of Russia and Greece, where they survive. The word comes from the Greek *eikon*, meaning "likeness," and strict rules were devised as to the subject, generally a saint, and to the form of the painting and its use, so although icon painting flourished in the 6th century it is extremely difficult to date icons painted then or later. A reaction to what was considered idolatry took place in the 8th century, resulting in **iconoclasm**, the destruction of such images.

iconography (1) The study and interpretation of representations in figurative art and their symbolic meanings
(also called **iconology**). It is particularly important in the
understanding of Christian art, especially of the medieval and Renaissance periods, e.g. the dove signifying
the Holy Spirit, or the fish symbolizing Christ. (2) The
album of etchings of his contemporaries by van DYCK.

Impasto An Italian word used to describe the thickness
and textures that can be achieved with ACRYLIC or OIL
PAINT.

Impressionism An art movement originating in France in
the 1860s, centred on a fairly diverse group of artists
who held eight exhibitions together between 1874 and
1886. The main artists were CÉZANNE, DEGAS, MANET,
MONET, MORISOT, Camille PISSARRO, RENOIR and SISLEY,
although they did not all show paintings at all eight exhibitions. The name of the movement was coined by critics
from a painting by Monet in the 1874 exhibition entitled
Impression: Soleil Levant. Members of the group were
variously influenced by the BARBIZON SCHOOL, the works
of TURNER and CONSTABLE and the realism of COURBET.
The advent of photography and scientific theories about
colour also had their impact on the painters' approach to
their work. The Impressionists were concerned with representing day-to-day existence in an objective and realistic manner, and they rejected the Romantic idea that a
painting should convey strong emotions. They wanted to
record the fleeting effects of light and movement, and so

their usual subjects were landscapes or social scenes like streets and cafes. They chose unusual viewpoints and painted "close-ups," probably influenced by photography. They were on the whole much freer in their use of unusual colours and a lighter palette; their subject matter was also less weighty, and they came in for some criticism over the lack of intellectual content of their painting. Impressionism has had an enormous influence on almost every subsequent major art movement: on CUBISM via Cézanne; on the synthetic art of GAUGUIN through SEURAT and the NEO-IMPRESSIONISTS, and on EXPRESSIONISM through the works of van GOGH. This influence has continued in a large proportion of 20th-century art.

Ingres, Jean-Auguste-Dominique (1780-1867) French painter, one of the greatest exponents of NEOCLASSICAL art. He studied at the Académie Royale in Toulouse and worked in DAVID's studio before winning the Prix de Rome in 1801 with *The Ambassadors of Agamemnon*. He was in Rome from 1806-24 and was greatly influenced by the works of RAPHAEL. His paintings during this period had variable receptions, and he earned his living with pencil portraits of French and English tourists. He returned to Paris in 1824, where he established his reputation with *The Vow of King Louis VIII*. From 1834-41 he was director of the French Academy in Rome and he later became a professor at the Ecole des Beaux-Arts in Paris. He presented a powerful opposition to the ROMANTICISM of DELACROIX and his circle, although some of his later portraits, e.g. *Mme Moitessier* (1851, 1856), and nudes, e.g. *The Turkish Bath* (1859-62), have an anatomical distortion and sensuousness of line that is not austerely classical. He strongly influenced DEGAS, PICASSO and MATISSE through his excellent draughtsmanship.

Inness, George (1825-94) American painter whose early landscapes were influenced by the HUDSON RIVER SCHOOL, as in *The Delaware Valley* (1865). He later adopted a freer, less detailed approach following a visit to Italy and to the BARBIZON SCHOOL in France. *The Monk* (1873) is impressionistic in its loosely painted dark masses and soft lights, while still retaining something of the mysticism of the Hudson River tradition. His work was widely admired in the US.

intaglio The cutting into a stone or other material or the etching or engraving on a metal plate of an image; the opposite of RELIEF. Intaglio printing techniques include ENGRAVING and ETCHING.

International Gothic A predominant style in European art covering the period between the end of the Byzantine era and the beginning of the RENAISSANCE, i.e. *c.*1375-*c.*1425. Some variations in styles occurred regionally, but the most influential centres were Italy, France and the Netherlands. Ideas spread widely due to an increase in the art trade, to travelling artists, and to a certain amount of rivalry over royal commissions. The Dukes of Berry and Burgundy were among the major patrons of the time. International Gothic style was characterized by decorative detail and refined, flowing lines; figures were often elongated or distorted to increase an appearance of elegant charm and the use of gilts and rich colours figured strongly. Scale and perspective were more symbolic than naturalistic, although naturalism began to take hold in the later works of the period, as in GENTILE DA FABRIANO's *Adoration of the Magi* (1423).

J

Jamesone, George (1581-1644) Scottish painter. The son of an Aberdeen architect, he studied under RUBENS in Antwerp, where van DYCK was a fellow pupil. In 1628 he returned to Scotland, where he became famous as a portrait painter although he also painted historical pieces and landscape. His work is noteworthy for the delicacy and softness of shading and a clear sense of colour.

Janssens, Abraham (1575-1632) Flemish painter. A contemporary of RUBENS, he lived and worked mainly in Antwerp, apart from one or two brief visits to Italy. His early works were MANNERIST in style, as in *Diana and Callisto* (1601), but later pieces are more classical in their clear modelling of figures and powerful lighting: *Scaldis and Antwerpia* (1609). His most memorable work is *Calvary* (c.1620). SEGHERS was his pupil.

Janssens *or* **Johnson, Cornelius** (1593-1664) English-born painter of Dutch parentage. He worked in England from 1618 to 1643 and was employed by James I and Charles I. His work, some of miniature size, includes portraits of these kings and of the poet John Milton as a boy. In 1643 he settled in Holland.

Jawlensky, Alexei von (1864-1941) Russian painter. He

lived in Munich from 1896 and was associated with
KANDINSKY and the BLAUE REITER group, although his
own style was more simply abstract with linear design
and flat areas of strong colour e.g. *Girl with Peonies*
(1909). From 1929 his works became more mystical, as
in the series *Night* (1933). His work was always of an independent nature, slightly removed from the trends of
the time.

Jazz Modern *see* **Art Deco**.

John, Augustus (1878-1961) English painter and
younger brother of Gwen JOHN. He studied at the Slade
School of Art, where he was an outstanding draughtsman
and became a champion of radical and revolutionary art.
He taught at the School of Art at University College,
Liverpool, for a time, but much of his life was spent in
nomadic journeyings in various parts of England, Ireland and Wales. A typical work of this period is *The Way
down to the Sea* (1909-11). He later visted Provence in
the South of France, producing a large number of oil
sketches: *Provencal Studies*. While the quality of his
work, especially his drawings, received intermittent
praise in the UK, he had 38 paintings exhibited in the
ARMORY SHOW of 1913, an indication of his stature
abroad. His innovations in painting were often misunderstood and maligned. *The Smiling Woman* (1908) and
Marchesa Casati (1919) are notable examples of his best
portraits.

John, Gwen (1876-1939) English painter and elder sister

of Augustus JOHN. She studied at the Slade School of Art and at WHISTLER's studio in Paris. She was a close friend of the sculptor, RODIN. A quiet and unassuming person, her paintings reflect her personality, sensitively painted in muted tones reminiscent of Whistler's palette. Her preferred subjects were young women in interior settings, and she creates a persuasive atmosphere of peace, stillness and quiet dignity, as in *A Lady Reading* (1907-8). In 1913 she converted to Roman Catholicism and lived in increasing seclusion at Meudon in France. She exhibited three paintings in the ARMORY SHOW of 1913, and her only one-man show was in London in 1926, but memorial and retrospective exhibitions held in 1946, 1952, 1968 and 1976 have done much to redress the balance of acclaim and appreciation she deserves.

Johns, Jasper (1930-) American painter, sculptor and printmaker. His early works are ABSTRACT EXPRESSIONIST pieces, but his style took on a new direction under the influences of RAUSCHENBERG and the composer John Cage. Famous among his avantgarde works are his *Target* and *Flag* paintings (1954-5), including *Target with Four Faces* (1955). His works, especially in sculpture, anticipate pop and conceptual art in its use of real objects. Some of his paintings incorporate objects like beer cans applied directly to the canvas. His mature works are more subtle in approach.

Johnson, Cornelius *see* **Janssen, Cornelius**.

Jordaens, Jacob (1593-1678) Flemish painter, engraver

and designer whose style was greatly influenced by his older contemporary RUBENS. He established a workshop in Antwerp in the 1620s, but he also assisted Rubens on major projects. Jordaens' own works include genre paintings, portraits and altarpieces, and he undertook large numbers of commissions including *The Triumph of Frederick Hendrick* (1652) for the Huis ten Bosch Villa at The Hague.

Jorn, Asger (1914-73) Danish painter and engraver. He studied in Paris and was involved with the Paris International Exhibition of 1937. Early influences include KLEE, ENSOR and AFRICAN tribal art. His works became more expressive in style during the 1940s. From 1955 he lived mainly in Paris. His paintings from the 1950s and 60s are vibrant and explosive in their powerful brushwork and colour, as in *Green Bullet* (1960).

Judd, Donald (1928-) American conceptual artist who studied at Columbia University and at the Art Students' League, New York. His geometric sculptures consist of painted cubes or other solid forms arranged in sequence on floors or low down on walls. His contention was that the shape, colour, volume or surface of an object were viable in themselves as works of art. He had his first one-man show at the Green Gallery in New York in 1964, and a retrospective at the Whitney Museum, New York, in 1968.

Jugendstil The German form of ART NOUVEAU. *See also* KIRCHNER; KLINGER.

Juni, Juan de (*c*.1510-77) Spanish sculptor who trained in Italy and Burgundy and settled at Valladolid in 1540. He was one of Spain's most important sculptors of the time. His style is expressive and graceful, and he executed a large number of sculptures on religious themes. Notable works include two representations of *The Entombment*, one at Valladolid, 1539-44, and one at Segovia Cathedral, 1571.

Justus of Ghent [Joos van Wassenhove] (*fl*.1460-80) Flemish artist. He was a member of the guilds of Antwerp and Ghent and a friend and contemporary of Hugo van der GOES. Notable among his early works are *The Crucifixion* and *The Adoration of the Magi*. He was in Italy from 1473-75, working for the Duke of Urbino, when he painted *The Communion of the Apostles* (1473-4); this work was to form an important link between the painting of Italy and The Netherlands.

K

Kandinsky, Wassily (1866-1944) Russian-born painter and art theorist who originally graduated in law from Moscow University before going to study painting in Munich in 1896. Typical of his early work is *Blue Mountain No. 84* (1908). He joined the Berlin SEZESSION in 1902, and returned to Berlin after a time travelling in Europe and Africa. By 1910 he was creating the beginnings of ABSTRACT EXPRESSIONISM, with non-figurative paintings whose significance depended on the interrelation of colours and forms. He formed the BLAUE REITER with Franz MARC before returning to Russia in 1918 to teach and to set up the Russian Academy of Artistic Sciences. With the imposition of social realism in Russia, Kandinsky returned to Germany in 1922, where he taught at the BAUHAUS until its closure in 1933. He then settled in France. Kandinsky's writings have been as influential as his paintings on 20th-century art, in particular *Reminiscences* (1913) and *Concerning the Spiritual in Art,* written in 1910, but not published until 1947. His ideas also spread to Europe and the US via a number of his exiled Bauhaus students.

Kane, Paul (1810-71) Irish-born Canadian painter. He

travelled in Canada for the Hudson Bay Company in the late 1840s and returned with an astonishing collection of sketches, which he used as a source for his bizarre paintings. He borrowed imaginatively from well-known European artists, as in *Blackfoot Chiefs*, where the composition is reminiscent of the works of RAPHAEL. Indian portraits painted by Kane bear an uncanny resemblance to the European aristocrats painted by REYNOLDS and RAEBURN. He published an account of his travels entitled *The Wanderings of an Artist* (1859), and by the time of his death had become something of a legend.

Kaprow, Allen (1927-) American artist, famous as the inventor of "happenings" [*see* ACTION PAINTING]. His earliest influences include ABSTRACT EXPRESSIONISM and the theories of chance and randomness expounded by the composer John Cage. In the late 1950s he began creating complicated assemblages and environmental pieces. The first happening took place in New York in 1959 and involved acted-out fantasies and responses by various "performers"; it was called *Eighteen happenings in six parts*. Kaprow has had an acknowledged influence on 20th-century art since the 1960s.

Kaufmann, Angelica (1741-1807) Swiss painter. Her early travels in Switzerland and Italy with her father engendered an appreciation of NEOCLASSICAL art, which she later applied to her work. She was in London from 1776 where she was a popular artist, doing portraits and scenes from Shakespeare and Homer as well as history paintings. She was a friend of REYNOLDS and a founder of the Royal Academy. She also decorated house interiors for architects like Robert ADAM. After her marriage in 1781 to the Italian landscape painter **Antonio Zucchi** (1726-95), she settled in Rome. Notable among her best portraits are those of the German writer Goethe and REYNOLDS.

Kelly, Ellsworth (1923-) American painter who studied in Boston and at the Académie des Beaux-Arts, Paris. He returned to the US in 1954, where he became a leading figure among the "hard-edge" group of ABSTRACT painters. His work consists of flat, bright areas of colour bounded by sharp edges, black and white geometric compositions, and panels of colour placed adjacently, e.g. *Blue, Green, Yellow, Orange, Red* (1966). He also did some sculptures and low-relief works along similar lines.

Kent, Rockwell (1882-1971) American painter and draughtsman. He trained in architecture at Columbia University, where he was a student of Robert HENRI and helped with the first Independents Show in 1910. His early landscapes owe something to the works of Winslow HOMER, although with more solidity of form and contrasting tones. The works of the EIGHT and the ASHCAN SCHOOL also had their influence, as in *The Road Roller* (1909). His black and white book illustrations are also well known and admired.

Keinholz, Edward (1927-) American sculptor. He studied in Washington and then went to Los Angeles where he opened the Now Gallery and the Ferus Gallery. He was initially a painter but moved on to three-dimensional constructions in the 1960s. His works are mainly tableaux built up with real objects and figures in plaster or other media. They are realist in approach, featuring some sordid aspects of society and illustrating his dislike of the superficial, materialistic side of American life. Notable works are *The State Hospital* (1966) and *Portable War Memorial* (1968).

kinetic art An art form in which light or balance are used to create a work that moves or appears to move. Kinetic artists include GABO, CALDER and CHADWICK. More complicated kinetic art objects are made to move by electric motors.

Kirchner, Ernst Ludwig (1880-1938) German painter and engraver. He studied at Dresden and Munich and was a founder of Die BRÜCKE. His initial works are in the *Jugendstil*, or German ART NOUVEAU manner, but he was also influenced by late Gothic German woodcuts, and this pervaded the works of Die Brücke. Other influences on Kirchner's early individual style were primitive art and the works of GAUGUIN and van GOGH, but his stylized drawing technique and strong juxtapositions of colours owe a great deal to the works of MUNCH and to MATISSE and the FAUVES. Kirchner's approach was impetuous and direct, concerned with expression of emotion, for which he developed personally symbolic images or "hieroglyphs" as a kind of pictorial language to describe emotions. Fears and anguish feature strongly in the years prior to World War I, and his woodcuts became more harsh and distorted. He suffered a nervous breakdown in 1914 and spent the rest of his life at a sanatorium. In the 1920s he painted more tranquil landscapes, but the last decade of his life saw a return to the abstract. Nazi condemnation of his work as "degenerate" sparked a return of mental illness, which led to his suicide.

Klee, Paul (1879-1940) Swiss painter. He studied in Munich and travelled in Italy before returning to his native Berne. By 1906 he was back in Munich, and in 1911 became involved with the BLAUE REITER, showing works in their second exhibition in 1912. Early works were influenced by CUBISM, ORPHISM and SYMBOLISM and were largely monochromatic, but the event that affected the character of much of his work was a trip to Tunisia with MACKE in 1914, which inspired a new approach to colour abstraction. He taught at the BAUHAUS and at the Dusseldorf Academy but was dismissed by the Nazis and returned to Berne in 1933. His work was included in the exhibition of allegedly "degenerate" art in 1937, and he suffered a severe depression thereafter. His later works are larger and darker and lack the joyful sparkle of earlier pieces, although his imaginative style and technical genius were undiminished. Through the outstanding quality of his own work and through his teaching, Klee has exerted an enormous influence on modern art, making him one of the most innovative and important artists of the 20th century.

Klimt, Gustav (1862-1918) Austrian painter who studied at the Vienna school of Arts and Crafts and was one of the founders of the Vienna SEZESSION. His early works were variously influenced by IMPRESSIONISM, SYMBOLISM and ART NOUVEAU, but were often misunderstood, and occasionally rejected by the commissioners, as happened with his murals for Vienna University (1900-3). He also exhibited at the Sezessions of 1903 and 1904 despite increasing controversy and isolation. One notable commission still in place is the mosaic mural for the Palais Stoclet in Brussels (1911). Klimt was an excellent draughtsman and had a great influence on younger artists such as KOKOSHKA and SCHIELE.

Kline, Franz (1910-62) American painter who studied in Boston and trained as a painter at the Heatherly School of Art in London. His earliest works were mainly city views and landscapes painted in heavy impasto, but from the 1950s he developed a style not unlike an enlarged and modified form of Chinese calligraphy. Working mainly in black and white, although he did experiment with colours, his paintings have an expressive fluidity of brushwork and boldly structured composition, as in *Chief* (1950) and *Ninth Street* (1951).

Klinger, Max (1857-1920) German painter, sculptor and illustrator. He studied at Karlsruhe and Berlin, travelling to Paris (1883-6) and Rome (1888-93) before settling in

Leipzig. His early training was in the classical tradition, which he adapted to his own development of ART NOUVEAU, and he is now thought of primarily as a *Jugendstil* or German ART NOUVEAU artist. His etchings contain elements of fantasy reminiscent of BÖCKLIN, which anticipate surrealist imagery, as in *Adventures of a Glove* (1881) and his illustrations to Brahms' *Fantasias*. His most famous sculpture is the Beethoven monument (1899-1902), and a noteworthy painting is *The Judgement of Paris* (1885-87).

Kokoshka, Oskar (1886-1980) Austrian painter who studied in Vienna where he met KLIMT and other SEZESSION artists and was influenced by ART NOUVEAU. A typical early work is the lithograph *The Dreaming Boys* (1908). He painted still lifes and a series of portraits renowned for a depth of insight into the personality of the sitter, whether innate or projected by the artist being a matter of debate; a typical example is *The Marquis of Montesquieu* (1909-10). He also did a number of graphic illustrations for *Die Sturm* magazine. He taught at the Dresden Academy until 1924 and then travelled around Europe and North Africa painting landscapes in an expressionist style and doing "portraits" of cities and towns from unusual viewpoints e.g. *Jerusalem* (1929-30). He moved to England in 1938 after the condemnation of his work by the Nazis; his painting *Self Portrait of a Degenerate Artist* (1937) is typical of the defiant eccentricity that characterizes much of his work.

Kollwitz, Käthe Schmidt (1867-1945) German engraver and sculptor. Her strong social convictions and compassion for the poor and oppressed in society are central to the import of her art (she was married to a doctor). Notable early works include *Weavers' Revolt* (1897-8) and *Peasants' War* (1902-8), two series of etchings that aroused considerable political controversy. *Mother and Child* was a common theme handled with sen-sitivity and gentleness in drawings and sculptures, e.g. *Pietà* (1903). Her pacifist views are evident in the lithograph cycles *The War* (1923) and *Death* (1934-5), which were in part the cause of her expul-sion from the Prussian Academy of Berlin in 1933.

Kuhn, Walt (1877-1949) American painter who studied in Paris and Munich and taught at the New York School of Art. He was associated with Robert HENRI and helped to organize the ARMORY SHOW of 1913. His earlier works are realist in approach, but in the 1920s and 30s the influences of PICASSO, DERAIN and MATISSE became more apparent. Favourite themes include circuses and clowns in bright colours, as well as landscapes and still lifes; a typical work is *Clown with Black Wig* (1930).

Kuniyoshi, Yasuo (1893-1953) Japanese-born American painter who studied art in Los Angeles and New York. He also earned a living as a photographer until his works achieved wider recognition in the 1930s after the Modern American Artists Exhibition of 1929. His works are decorative, full of symbolic imagery and reminiscent of naive art in depth and perspective. A typical work is *I'm Tired* (1938). His works became extremely popular in Japan during the 1960s.

Kupka, Frank (1871-1957) Czech painter. He studied in Prague and Vienna and worked as an illustrator in Paris, where he lived from 1895. He was associated with Marcel DUCHAMP and became interested in the problems of depicting movement, which he explored in the series *Girl with a Ball* (1908). He continued the same theme in *Amorpha, Fugue in Two Colours* (1912), which was an innovation in the development of ABSTRACT painting. ORPHISM also influenced his work in terms of its mysticism. A notable piece in his mature style is *Working Steel* (1921-29), conveying a sense of the power and movement of the machine age.

L

Lachaise, Gaston (1882-1935) French sculptor who studied in Paris and settled in the US in 1906. He had his first one-man show at the Bourgeois Gallery, New York, in 1918. He was responsible for renewing enthusiasm for direct carving methods in American sculpture, and his work represents a move away from academic forms and strictures. He was known for his perceptive portrait busts and for his female figure studies. These were large and smoothly articulated with a voluptuous femininity reminiscent of the paintings of Renoir, e.g. *Standing Woman* (1912-27).

Lafarge, John (1835-1910) American painter. He studied in Paris and derived his influences from a variety of sources, including oriental art. His first major commission was to decorate Trinity Church, Boston, where he devised murals and stained glass windows. He was associated with William MORRIS and the PRE-RAPHAELITE movement in his approach to art. Notable works include *Maua—our Boatman* (1891).

Landseer, Sir Edwin (1802-73) English painter of precocious talent who was a student of HAYDON and won acclaim while still a child for his animal drawings, including the Society of Art silver palette at age 11. His

etchings and paintings were technically very well observed and draughted, but tended towards a gross senti-
mentality in humanizing animals, particularly dogs, e.g
The Old Shepherd's Chief Mourner (1937), a quality that
was the source of his widespread popularity throughout
his career. He was Queen Victoria's favourite painter,
and his works were well known through engraved copies. Other notable works include *The Monarch of the
Glen* (1850), and the the lions modelled for Trafalgar
Square in 1867.

Lascaux The site, in Dordogne, France, of some outstanding paleolithic cave paintings and rock engravings. Dating from *c*.15000BC, they have survived in remarkably
good condition and depict local fauna etc., on a large
scale and in a bold, direct style.

La Tour, Georges (1593-1652) French painter who
worked in Luneville under the patronage of the Duke of
Lorraine. Around 40 of his works have survived, but
only two are dated, which complicates any assessment of
his artistic development. He was strongly influenced by
CARAVAGGIO, and probable early works include *Peasant*
and *Peasant's Wife* (*c*.1620). These feature strong, dramatic lighting, whereas those thought to be later paintings have a monumental air of stillness with figures lit
by a single candle, e.g.*St Sebastian tended by the Holy
Women* (*c*.1650). La Tour's works are possessed of a
more classical serenity than the late MANNERIST paintings
of his contemporaries.

Lavery, Sir John (1856-1941) Irish-born Scottish painter and member of the GLASGOW SCHOOL. He studied in Paris and *plein-air* painting had a strong influence on his work. WHISTLER was another major influence, as is evident in Lavery's commissions celebrating the visit of Queen Victoria to the Glasgow International Exhibition of 1888. His well-draughted compositions are light and relaxed in atmosphere, e.g. *The Tennis Party* (1885). The main output of his later career was in portraiture.

Lawrence, Jacob (1917-) American painter, he trained at FEDERAL ART PROJECTS classes and was an important figure in highlighting social problems drawn out of Black culture in the 1930s. Major works include the 60 paintings in a series entitled *The Migration of the Negro* (1940-41).

Lawrence, Sir Thomas (1769-1830) English painter, mainly self-taught. He established his reputation at the age of twenty with a commissioned portrait of *Queen Charlotte* (1789), and quickly became the leading portraitist of his time. He succeeded REYNOLDS as King's Painter in 1792. A notable achievement is the series of 24 full-length portraits of the military leaders after the battle of Waterloo (1818). His work rises out of 18th-century traditions but with a fluidity and sparkle that anticipates the ROMANTICISM of the 19th century.

Lebrun, Charles (1619-90) French painter, he trained with Simon VOUET and worked in POUSSIN's studio in Rome. Returning to Paris in 1646, he established himself in decorative murals doing vigorous and grandiose illusionistic paintings, such as the ceiling of the gallery at the Hotel Lambert. He was a fine draughtsman and portraitist, and was court painter to Louis XIV from 1661. He was responsible for much of the decor of Versailles, including the Galérie des Glaces (1679-84) and the Great Staircase (1671-8), since destroyed. In 1663 he became director of the Gobelins factory and designed the famous tapestry *Louis XIV visiting the Gobelins* (1663-75). He was also director of the Academy of Art, and established the basis of a powerful academic tradition, devolved from the CLASSICISM of Poussin, the theory of which he published in a treatise in 1698.

Léger, Fernand (1881-1955) French painter. His early works were strongly influenced by CUBISM and he was a member of the SECTION D'OR group from 1910-1914. His early paintings and most of his figurative works involve simplifications of form and structure resulting in static, rather tubular figure forms, as in *Nude in the Forest* (1909-10). He subsequently began to introduce mechanical forms and reflective metallic surfaces into his work, e.g. *Contrasting Forms* (1913, one of a series), and in-creasingly derived his imagery from the machine. Later works are again more figurative and monumental, as in his large-scale paintings, *The Builders* (1950) and *The Great Parade* (1954).

Lehmbruck, Wilhelm (1881-1919) German sculptor and illustrator who studied at Dusseldorf and Paris. He was greatly influenced by RODIN's EXPRESSIONISM, although his own work contains elements of the classical smoothness of MAILLOL and the graceful, stylized distortions of Gothic sculpture, e.g. *Kneeling Woman* (1911). Along with BARLACH, he played an influential role in the revival of sculpture in Germany at the beginning of the 20th century.

Lely, Sir Peter [Pieter van der Faes] (1618-80) Dutchborn English painter who trained at Haarlem and moved to England *c.*1643. His early works are landscapes and historical paintings, but he soon turned to portrait painting, in which he was greatly influenced by van DYCK. He lacked van Dyck's flair for elegance, and his approach was generally more superficial, but he set a trend for society portrait styles, which continued for nearly a century. He painted most of the court of Charles II, e.g. the two series *The Windsor Beauties* and *Maids of Honour*. He was knighted in 1680.

Le Nain, Antoine (*c.*1588-1648), **Louis** (*c.*1593-1648) and **Matthieu** (1607-77) French painters. Brothers from Laon, they established a studio in Paris from *c.*1630, and were founder members of the Academy. The fact that they all signed their works without initials has created an element of uncertainty in attributing which to whom, but it is generally accepted that Louis was the most important of the three, creating simple and dignified genre paintings of peasant life, e.g. *The Peasant's Meal* (1642). Of the other two brothers, Antoine painted small works and miniatures, e.g. *The Little Singers*, and Matthieu painted portraits and larger pictures, e.g. *The Guardroom* (1643). All three collaborated on religious paintings.

Leonardo da Vinci (1452-1519) Florentine painter, draughtsman, engineer, musician and thinker; the outstanding genius of his time, and of many others. He trained in the studio of VERROCCHIO, where he probably painted the left-hand angel in Verrocchio's *Baptism of Christ* (*c*.1472). Verrocchio was reputedly impressed to the extent that he gave up painting. Leonardo was a painstaking worker and evolved a technique of thin glazes of oil paint to build up an image of extraordinary translucence and detail, e.g. the far distance landscapes in *The Annunciation* . His use of this technique was to prove disastrous for the mural of *The Last Supper* (1489) in the refectory of San Maria del Grazie, Milan, which began to deteriorate within his own lifetime. He was also ambitious in his compositions, although somewhat dilatory in their execution, so that many of his works remained unfinished, e.g. *The Adoration of the Magi* (commissioned 1881, not completed). In 1483 he wrote recommending himself to Duke Sforza of Milan as an engineer and a musician. While in Milan he painted the two versions of *The Virgin of the Rocks*, which demonstrate the subtle modelling of light and shade between figures and background, known as *sfumato*. This represented a remarkable departure from the RENAISSANCE art stress on strong lighting and outline. Leonardo's works

had a profound influence on the art of RAPHAEL and
PERUGINO. He also began the Sforza Monument, an
equestrian statue for which he only completed the horse,
which was later destroyed. Leonardo left Milan in 1499
and travelled between Florence and Rome, where he
painted the *Mona Lisa* (*c*.1505) for Giulio de' MEDICI.
He also composed the beautiful cartoon of *The Virgin
and St Anne* (1504-6), which he exhibited as a work of
art in its own right. He was always more interested in de-
vising the composition of a work, in developing character and gesture, than in completion; his creative ingenuity was always pursuing some new idea. With Leonardo
originates the view of the artist as a creative thinker and
not merely a skilled artisan. In 1516 he was invited to
France by King Francis I, and he remained there until his
death. His later years were devoted to scientific studies,
and he completed no more major paintings, although his
drawings for other projects were prolific and beautiful.
Leonardo's influence on art and science in his own and
succeeding generations was colossal and vitrually un-
matched up to the present day.

Lewis, Percy Wyndham (1882-1957) English painter
and author. He was a leader of the short-lived Vorticist
movement and major contributor and editor of the two
issues of its magazine, *Blast* (1914), in which he advo-
cated a departure from traditional Victorian values. His
use of violent colour and severe angularity in his paintings is reminiscent of Italian FUTURISM. Using reiterated

forms suggestive of the machine age, he created some of the earliest virtually abstract works, e.g. *Workshop* (1914). Later works include some outstanding portraits, notably that of *T.S. Eliot* (1938).

Lewitt, Sol (1928-) American sculptor whose work centres on the infinite variety of combinations of simple geometric forms. He developed series of arrangements of two- and three-dimensional images and grid projections in monochrome, e.g. *Open Modular Cube* (1966). Later pieces included the three primary colours also.

Leyden, Lucas van (1494-1533) Dutch painter and engraver. He was a child prodigy, producing mature, accomplished works from the age of 14, e.g. *Mohammed and the Murdered Monk* (1508). He was greatly influenced by DÜRER, but his subject matter is more diverse and the quality of his prolific output less consistent although often outstanding in originality. He had a large and widespread influence on other painters. Other notable works include *The Game of Chess* (*c.*1510), *The Card Players* (*c.*1516) and the *Last Judgement* triptych (1526-27), which was his masterpiece.

Lichtenstein, Roy (1923-) American painter, graphic artist and sculptor. He initially worked in commercial art, and his early paintings are in the ABSTRACT EXPRESSIONIST tradition, but he is best known as a protagonist of pop art. He draws his imagery from comic strip magazines, blowing up single frames and reproducing the enlarged dot matrix by hand, e.g. *Whaam!* (1963) and *As I Opened Fire* (1963).

Liebermann, Max (1847-1935) German painter and graphic artist. He studied in Berlin and Weimar, and came under the influence of the BARBIZON SCHOOL while travelling in France and Holland. He was influential in promoting new Impressionist ideas in German art, and was a founder of the Berlin SEZESSION in 1898. He was also president of the Berlin Academy from 1922 to 1933. Although his work was declared degenerate by the Nazis, he finally came to represent the formal traditionalism that artists, such as those of Die BRÜCKE, later reacted against.

Limbourg, Jean, Paul and **Herman** (all *fl.* 1400-16) Dutch illuminators. They worked on Biblical texts for Philip, Duke of Burgundy, until his death in 1404. They then went into the service of his brother Jean, Duke of Berry, for whom they produced the *Belles Heures* (*c.*1408). A second manuscript, *Les Tres Riches Heures*, which was unfinished at the time of their deaths, represents the major work of their career. It is an outstanding example of the INTERNATIONAL GOTHIC style, and surpasses contemporary accomplishments in its complex composition and landscape detail.

Lipchitz, Jacques (1891-1973) Russian sculptor. He originally trained as an engineer before settling in Paris in 1909, when he began to study art. His early work is concerned with the three-dimensional potential CUBIST ideas, based on interlocking planes, e.g. *Head* (1915). Later works are more linear and surrealist in approach, but he returned to his Cubist principles after settling in the US in 1941. Notable works include *Sacrifice* (1948).

Lippi, Filippino (1457-1504) Florentine painter, son of Filippo LIPPI, he trained in BOTTICELLI's studio, where he became an excellent draughtsman. His style is bolder and more vigorous than that of Botticelli, as in his first important painting *The Vision of St Bernard* (*c*.1480). His most outstanding works are his frescoes, in particular *The Life of St Thomas Aquinas* (1488-93) for Santa Maria sopra Minerva in Rome, and *The Lives of Saints Philip and John* (1495-1502) in Santa Maria Novella, Florence.

Lippi, Fra Filippo (*c*.1406-69) Florentine painter. He took up painting under the influence of MASACCIO, who had decorated the Brancacci Chapel in the Carmine monastery where Filippo was a monk. He later forsook his vows in order to marry the mother of his son, Filppino LIPPI. Early works reveal the influence of Masaccio, although without the same strength of form or light, e.g. *Annunciation* . However, his style gradually became more lyrical and fluid, investing his paintings with a certain wistful melancholy and naive charm, e.g. *Adoration in the Wood* . He was one of the first to explore and develop the *Madonna and Child* theme, and most of his work was innovative both in style and subject.

Lombardo, Pietro (*c*.1435-1515) Venetian sculptor, father of **Tullio** (*c*.1455-1532) and **Antonio** (*d*.1516), with whom he ran a family workshop producing decorations and monuments for chapels in Venice, Padua and Treviso. Pietro executed the monument to *Doge Pietro Mocenigo* (*c*.1476-81) and was also the architect for the Church of Santa Maria dei Miracoli in Venice. Tullio's style is more fluid and sensual, e.g. the *Adam* from the *Vendramin* Monument (1439). Antonio's work is less well documented, but he collaborated with his brother on a number of commissions, notably *St Anthony's Shrine* (*c*.1500).

Lorenzetti, Ambrogio, and **Pietro** (both *fl.* 1320-48) Sienese painters and brothers, they probably trained under DUCCIO, although they developed a style that shows the influence of GIOTTO in the fullness of form and the depth of perspective in their works. Typical of Pietro's works are the early polyptych altarpiece *The Virgin and Child with Saints* (1320) and the later *Birth of the Virgin* (*c*.1342). Ambrogio was particularly skilled in his use of perspective, as in his most important work, the fresco series on *Good and Bad Government* (1338-39) for the Palazzo Pubblico in Siena.

Lotto, Lorenzo (*c*.1480-1556) Venetian painter and contemporary of TITIAN and GIORGIONE, he probably trained in the studio of Giovanni BELLINI, who influenced his early works. His career was idiosyncratic and his successes inconsistent, His best works are probably his portraits, which have a disturbing quality of intensity and unusual modes of colour and composition, e.g. *Young Man in his Study* (*c.*1528). Other notable works include *The Crucifixion* (1531). In later life his eyesight deteriorated and he spent his last years in the monastery at Loreto as a lay brother.

Louis, Morris (1912-62) American painter. His early influences include CUBISM and EXPRESSIONISM, but in 1954 he saw *Mountains and Sea* by Helen FRANKENTHALER, and pioneered techniques in colour stain painting. This method of pouring thin washes of colour on to unprimed, or even unstretched, canvas afforded him a means of avoiding the gestural marks and surface textures of expressionist painting. His major works were series paintings, notably the *Veil* series, e.g. *Vav* (1960), and the *Unfurled* series, e.g. *Alpha-phi* (1961).

Lowry, L[aurence] S[tephen] (1887-1976) English painter from Salford, near Manchester, his main employment was as a clerk for a property company, and he trained at art classes only intermittently between 1905 and 1925. He evolved a highly idiosyncratic painting style, mainly of urban industrial environments populated by matchstick-style figures. His paintings convey an intense atmosphere of human loneliness and alienation. Although he had an important exhibition in the Reid-Lefevre Gallery, London, in 1939, his work only achieved wider recognition in the Arts Council Retrospective Exhibition of 1966. A major retrospective was held at the Royal Academy in 1976. Critical opinion of his stature is widely divergent.

Luks, George Benjamin (1867-1933) American painter and graphic artist. He studied at the Pennsylvania Academy and became a member of The EIGHT and the ASHCAN SCHOOL under the influence of Robert HENRI. His style is flamboyant and vigorous, and his subject matter is concerned with social and urban realism. Much of his work reveals his indebtedness to Henri and also to MANET. Notable among his paintings is *The Wrestlers* (1905).

M

Mabuse, Jean de *see* **Gossaert, Jan**.

Macdonald-Wright, Stanton (1890-1973) American painter who was a co-founder of SYNCHROMISM, a movement in colour abstraction along similar lines to ORPHISM. Macdonald-Wright's paintings tended to have a representational motif, e.g *Sunrise Synchromy in Violet* (1918). In 1919 he settled in California where he taught art and experimented in colour film. After 1937 he became interested in Zen and travelled annually to Japan. His later Synchromist paintings indicate the influence of oriental art.

Mackintosh, Charles Rennie *see* **Art Nouveau**.

Macke, August (1887-1914) German painter and founder member of Der BLAUE REITER, his early influences include FAUVISM and CUBISM, e.g. *Church in Bonn* (1911). He exhibited with Der Blaue Reiter in 1911. Subsequent works are coloured by the influences of ORPHISM, e.g. *Walk on the Bridge* (1911) and by the powerful atmospheric light of North Africa. Macke's works had a powerful influence on Paul KLEE.

McTaggart, William (1835-1910) Scottish painter, sometimes referred to as the Scottish Impressionist, al-

though his magnificent sky- and seascapes are closer to
the ideas and aspirations of Constable in their depiction
of changing light and cloud movement. He is renowned
for having painted mainly out of doors and in all weath-
ers. His works are freely and powerfully painted, conveying the breathtaking shock of strong winds and
stormy seas and skies.

Maes, Nicolaes (1634-93) Dutch painter from Dordrecht.
He studied with Rembrandt, and his early genre works
show the deep influence of his teacher in his rich palette
of reds and browns and in contrasts of light and shade,
e.g. *The Listening Maid* (1656). After the mid-1660s his
style changed. He began to paint portraits more in the
style of van Dyck, and his palette became cooler and
greyer. He moved to Amsterdam in 1673, where he became a successful society portraitist. His work had a
strong influence on succeeding generations of portrait
painters.

maestà The Italian word for "majesty," used in art to denote a depiction of the Virgin and Child enthroned in
majesty and surrounded by angels or saints.

Magritte, René (1898-1967) Belgian painter. His early
styles included Impressionism and Cubism, but he became interested in Surrealism after seeing *Song of Love*
(1922) by de Chirico. He was involved with the production of the Dadaist publication *Oesophage,* and painted
his first Surrealist works, e.g *The Menaced Assassin*
(1926), from about 1925. He had links with the French

Surrealists, including BRETON and DALI while living near Paris between 1927 and 1930.

Maillol, Aristide (1861-1944) French sculptor, designer and painter. He initially worked in tapestry design and was a succesful painter, but took up sculpture when his eyesight began to deteriorate. He is best remembered for his sculptures of the female nude in the classical and idgnified style of Greek and Roman sculpture, e.g. *The Mediterra-nean* (*c.*1901). His sculptural works were highly influential.

Malevich, Kasimir Severinovich (1878-1935) Russian painter of Polish origins, his early works, such as T*he Knife Grinder* (1912), combine the influences of CUBISM and FUTURISM. From around 1915 he pioneered SUPREMATIST ideas of purely abstract art, sometimes anticipating the Minimalist art of the 1960s, e.g. *Black Square* (1915) and the series *White on White* (*c.*1918). From 1919 he taught at the Vitebsk School of Art, where he championed Suprematist theories over those of CONSTRUCTIVISM. His later works revert to an earlier interest in genre themes, and he produced some notable portraits of his friends and family.

Manet, Edouard (1832-83) French painter. He derived much of his inspiration from the Old Masters and from the Spanish painters VELAZQUEZ and RIBERA. He established early success at the Salon with *The Guitarist* (1861). Subsequent paintings, however, such as *Le Déjeuner sur l'Herbe* (1863) and *Olympia* (1863), caused outrage due to his direct approach and fresh, painterly style. The public could not accept his use of contemporary figures and settings, and the critics objected to the direct, bold lighting that reduced mid-tone modelling of the figures. The subjects derive from older paintings: GIORGIONE's *Concert Champêtre* and TITIAN's *Venus d'Urbino*. Manet was by no means a willing leader of the avant-garde, and although his pupils and associates, such as DEGAS and MORISOT, were IMPRESSIONISTS, he himself never exhibited with them. They did encourage him to paint out of doors, and his later works have a lighter, freer atmosphere, e.g. *Argenteuil* (1874). He sketched much of the subject matter of his late paintings, e.g. *Bar aux Folies Bergères* (1881) in Parisian cafes. His paintings won increasing acceptance, and he was awarded the Légion d'Honneur in 1881. His work had a widespread and profound influence on 20th-century painting.

Mannerism An exaggerated and often artificial sense of style found in Italian art between *c.*1520 and 1600, i.e. between the High RENAISSANCE and BAROQUE periods. It represents a reaction against the balanced forms and perspectives of Renaissance art and is characterized by uncomfortably posed, elongated figures and contorted facial expressions. Harsh colours and unusual modes of perspective were also used to striking effect. The major artists of the period, e.g. PONTORMO and Giovanni BOLOGNA, were able to create emotional responses of greater power and sophistication, and they paved the way for the development of Baroque art.

Mantegna, Andrea (*c*.1430-1506) Italian painter and prominent figure of the early RENAISSANCE, who was the brother-in-law of Giovanni BELLINI. A proficient draughtsman, he had the rare ability for that time of being skilled in the use of perspective, and he used his knowledge of classical antiquity in his frescoes for the Eremetani church in Padua (1448-57), since mainly destroyed. One of his major works that made full use of illusionistic perspective was the decor for the bridal chamber of the Ducal Palace in Mantua. It depicts groups of visitors to the palace, along with court figures, in a setting that seems to extend the space of the room and open out the ceiling to the sky. His mastery of foreshortening is fully expressed in the *trompe l'oeil* figures looking down from a ceiling balcony. Among his late works are the masterpieces depicting the *Triumph of Caesar* (1486-94), nine canvases commissioned by Francesco Gonzago. Mantegna also introduced the art of engraving on copper into northern Italy, and the engravings of his works earned him widespread popularity and influenced the art of Bellini and Dürer. He was greatly revered in his own lifetime, and his stature in art history remains undiminished.

Maratti, Carlo (1625-1713) Italian painter. He trained with SACCHI, and became a proficient portrait painter, e.g. *Pope Clement IX* (1667-69). His best works were influenced by the calm, classical tradition of RAPHAEL, in contrast to the Baroque dynamism of his contemporaries. He established an early successful career with works such as *The Adoration of the Shepherds* and *Madonna and Child* (c.1695). Due to his successes, his work was much imitated, and his achievements subsequently declined as his paintings became less distinguish-able from those of his followers.

Marc, Franz (1880-1916) German EXPRESSIONIST painter, one of the leading members of Der BLAUE REITER. He studied in Munich and was in Paris from 1903 to 1906; early influences include IMPRESSIONISM and the works of van GOGH. From 1908 he began making small animal figures in bronze, and developed a personally symbolic colour system in his works, e.g. *The Blue Horse* (1911). Along with KANDINSKY, he formed the New Artists Association in 1910, and then der Blaue Reiter in 1911. Later works, influenced by DELAUNAY and CUBISM, are more abstract although still powerfully symbolic, e.g. *Fighting Forms* (1913). Marc was killed fighting in World War I.

Marsh, Reginald (1898-1954) American painter. He worked as an illustrator for *Harper's Bazaar* and *The New Yorker* and painted seriously from about 1923. He painted the tawdry, downbeat side of city life in the Depression of the 1930s, contrasting it with the contentment of the rich. His work was therefore in the social-realist tradition, and suggests the influence of German

NEUE SACHLICHKEIT. Typical works include *The Park Bench* (1933) and *Pip and Flip* (1932).

Masaccio, [Tommaso di Ser Giovanni di Mone] (1401-c.1428) Florentine painter, a key figure of the early RENAISSANCE. His earliest dated work, the San Giovenale triptych (1422), portrays *The Madonna and Child with Saints*, painted with revolutionary realism. The figures and the throne are solidly modelled, with all the weight and auth-ority of a sculpture, revealing Masaccio's indebtedness to DONATELLO. Masaccio is properly the heir to GIOTTO in his rejection of Gothic elegance and decorative detail, and his development of perspective is informed by the architecture of BRUNELLESCHI. His most important surviving masterpieces are the Pisa polyptych (1426), the Brancacci Chapel frescoes, particularly those on *The Life of St Peter*, in Santa Maria del Carmine, Florence, and the *Trinity* fresco (*c.*1428) in Santa Maria Novella, Florence.

Masolino da Panicale (*c.*1383-1447) Florentine painter. He trained under GHIBERTI and was influenced by GENTILE DA FABRIANO. His early work is in the fluid, elegant style of INTERNATIONAL GOTHIC, as in the idealized and decorative *Madonna and Child* (1423). Subsequent works, such as *The Crucifixion* from the San Clemente frescoes (1428-31) in Rome, were influenced by the solid, sculptural painting style of MASACCIO; Masolino collaborated with him on the frescos for the Brancacci Chapel of Santa Maria del Carmine in Florence (*c.*1425-

28). Later works revert to a more Gothic style of decorative line, although he maintained a sense of pictorial space and perspective.

Masson, André (1896-1987) French painter, one of the circle of SURREALISTS that included BRETON, MIRÓ and ERNST. He established techniques of "automatic" linear drawings based on the expression of the subconcious. Paintings were developed incorporating pigments, sand and adhesive. He broke away from the Surrealist group in the late 1920s, and his later works have a mythological symbolism with imagery derived from Spanish bullfights or from nature, e.g. M*editations on an Oak Leaf* (1942).

Master of Flemalle, *see* **Campin, Robert**.

Matisse, Henri (1869-1954) French painter who studied law before beginning art classes in 1892. Early influences include the NEO-IMPRESSIONISM of SIGNAC. At the Salon d'Automne in 1905 he exhibited, along with DERAIN and VLAMINCK, the fresh, brightly coloured works that earned them the soubriquet "FAUVES." He continued to paint more abstract and decorative works, emphasizing the flat picture plane rather than spatial depth and volume, e.g. *Joie de Vivre* (1906). Subsequent works were more austere and formal, e.g. *Bathers by a River* (1916-17) although he gradually developed a more naturalistic style in his series of *Odalisques* (1920s). Despite serious illness, his late works are joyful and brightly coloured. He made use of cut-outs and COLLAGE in simple compositions , e.g. *Escargot*. Notable sculptures include *Back I-IV* (1909-30), and he designed the Chapel of the Rosary at Vence (1949-51), including ceramic tiles and vestments, as a gift for the nuns who cared for him during his illness.

Maurer, Alfred Henry (1868-1932) American painter. His early paintings are naturalistic in the IMPRESSIONIST style, but from 1908 he began to experiment more under the influence of FAUVISM, and his late works show an interest in CUBISM. He exhibited in the ARMORY SHOW of 1913. His potential was somewhat stifled by the conservatism of his father, who was a lithographer. Maurer committed suicide shortly after his father's death. Typical works include *Still Life with Fish* (1927-28).

Mauve, Anton (1838-88) Dutch painter, prominent leader of The Hague School. He painted small, delicately lit landscapes which show the influence of COROT and MILLET. His work was popular, and he was admired by his nephew van GOGH, whom he encouraged to paint. His work is well represented in Dutch collections and abroad, e.g. *Scheveningen* (1874).

Medici Italian family, political rulers of Florence in the 15th century and dukes of Tuscany from the 16th century to 1737. They were important patrons of the arts throughout their dynasty. Artists who came under their patronage at various times included DONATELLO, BRUNELLESCHI, Fra ANGELICO, Fra Filippo LIPPI and his son Filippino, MICHELANGELO, VERROCCHIO, RAPHAEL,

VASARI and BOLOGNA. Cosimo I de' Medici [Cosimo the Elder] began the great art collection now in the Uffizi, Florence.

medium A material used in art, e.g. oil in painting, pencil in drawing, or bronze in sculpture. The term is also used to denote a method, e.g. painting as opposed to sculpture.

Memling *or* **Memlinc, Hans** (*c*.1430/40-1494) German-born Dutch painter, probably a pupil of Rogier van der WEYDEN. His works are influenced by his master in terms of subject and composition, but they have a calmer, more serene quality in contrast to van der Weyden's emotional intensity. He was a prolific and popular artist and carried on a successful career as a portraitist. Notable works include *Tommaso Portinari and his Wife* (*c*.1468).

Mengs, Anton Raffael (1728-1779) German painter prominent in the NEOCLASSICAL movement. He was taught by his father and achieved success with his portraits, becoming court painter from 1745. In 1761 he was invited to Spain, where his portraits and ceilings for the royal palaces were preferred to those of his rival, TIEPOLO. With the exception of the Parnassus ceiling painting in the Villa Albani in Rome, his portraits were more noteworthy than his frescoes. He expounded his theories in *Considerations on Beauty and Taste in Painting* (1672).

Metaphysical Painting An art movement begun in Italy

in 1917 by CARRÀ and de CHIRICO. They sought to portray the world of the subconscious by presenting real objects in incongruous juxtaposition, as in their *Metaphysical Interiors* and *Muses* series (1917). Carrà abandoned the movement after a very short time, and by the early 1920s both artists had developed other interests. Although short-lived, the movement did have some influence on other artists of the time.

Michelangelo Buonarotti (1475-1564) Florentine painter, sculptor, draughtsman, architect and poet, an outstanding figure in art history and influential genius of the Italian RENAISSANCE. He trained in Florence with GHIRLANDAIO. Lorenzo the Magnificent [de MEDICI] was one of his early patrons. In Rome from 1496-1501 he established his reputation with the sculptures *Bacchus* (1496-7) and *Pietà* (1499). The fresco of *The Battle of Cascina*, commissioned in 1501 for the Palazzo Vecchio, was not completed, but before returning to Rome he executed the powerful sculpture of *David* (1501-4) for the Florentine Council. From 1505 Pope Julius II was his patron, and it was he who commissioned the ceiling paintings for the Sistine Chapel (1508-12), Michelangelo's great and lasting achievement. The upper part of the ceiling contains images from the book of Genesis, lower down are the prophets and sybils, and the lunettes and spandrels portray characters from the ancestry of Christ and the Virgin. The *Last Judgment* fresco (1536-41) on the altar wall was a much later addition and reflects the pessimism of the artist and a post-Reformation obsession with wrath and punishment. The intervening time was spent working in the Medici Chapel, San Lorenzo, on the tombs of Lorenzo and Giuliano de Medici. Much of his later life was taken up with the rebuilding of St Peter's, but notable later works include the unfinished *Rondanini Pietà* and a series of drawings of the Holy family and the Crucifixion for Vittorio Colonna. Michelangelo's art inspired and affected his contemporaries and subsequent generations of painters with incalculable effects up to the present day.

Millais, Sir John Everett (1829-96) English painter. A child prodigy, he studied at the Royal Academy Schools where he met Holman HUNT and, along with ROSSETTI, they founded the PRE-RAPHAELITE BROTHERHOOD. They embraced a philosophy of truth to nature and attention to detail, chosing themes that embodied strongly poetic or moral sentiment. The results often involved posed, studio tableaux in clashing colours, and the Pre-Raphaelites were unpopular with the critics until championed by John RUSKIN, whose wife Millais later married. Millais gradually achieved success and later abandoned his Pre-Raphaelite style. He became President of the Royal Academy in 1896 and painted the portraits of many prominent politcal figures, including *Gladstone* and *Carlyle*. Other notable works are *Bubbles* (1886) and *The Boyhood of Raleigh* (1870).

Milles, Carl (1875-1955) Swedish sculptor who studied

in Paris and Munich and was influenced by RODIN. He experimented with various styles, which he incorporated in his work. He was professor of the academy at Stockholm and also taught in the US. Notable works include the Peace Monument (1936) and the Orpheus Fountain (1930-36).

Millet, Jean-François (1814-75) French painter who studied at Cherbourg before winning a scholarship in 1837 to train in Paris. He earned his living by portraiture and exhibited his first major genre painting, *The Winnower*, at the Salon in 1848. He lived at BARBIZON on the edge of the Fontainebleau Forest from 1849, and his pastoral scenes developed a strong sense of realism. In 1850 he exhibited *The Sower* along with works by COURBET at the Salon, and he was labelled a social-realist although his works had no political motive. From the 1860s he painted more direct landscapes.

Miró, Joan (1893-1983) Spanish painter, sculptor and designer, his early works were influenced by DADA, CUBISM and Catalan art. *Catalan Landscape* (1923) marks the beginning of his SURREALIST style. From the late 1920s, his works are characterized by simplified, brightly coloured forms, free-floating against a plain background; a dream world more whimsically abstract and humourous than the works of his contemporaries, DALI and MAGRITTE. Notable among his works are the *Sun Wall* and *Moon Wall* murals (1958) for the UNESCO building in Paris, and his *Constellation* series (1940). His sculp-

tural works were highly inventive and linked to the imagery of his paintings.

mobile *see* **Calder, Alexander**.

Modigliani, Amadeo (1884-1920) Italian painter and
sculptor, his early training was in Florence and Naples but
from 1906 he lived and worked mainly in Paris and little
of his Italian work has survived. Influenced by BRANCUSI,
he took up sculpture and created naive, powerful figures
and heads inspired by AFRICAN and primitive art, e.g.
Head (*c*.1911-12). His paintings, mainly portraits, were
influenced by CÉZANNE and PICASSO, e.g. *Jeanne
Hebuterne* (1919), and reached a peak of simplification of
form and refinement of line and colour in the last decade
of his life.

Moholy-Nagy, Laszlo (1895-1946) Hungarian-born
painter and sculptor. He trained in Hungary and was initially influenced by CUBISM. In 1920 he moved to Berlin
and was subsequently inspired by CONSTRUCTIVISM. In
1922 he exhibited metal sculptures in his first one-man
show. Later pieces involve the use of transparent
sheeting and film to organize space. From 1923 he was
head of metalwork at the BAUHAUS and began to experiment with film and with light-sensitive paintings, or
"photograms". He left the Bauhaus in 1928 and worked
in Paris, Amsterdam and London as a photographer and
designer. He lived in Chicago from 1937 and directed
the New Bauhaus, later the Institute of Design, until his
death. His importance lies in his pioneering experimen-

tation and in his influence as a teacher. He published his treatise, *The New Vision*, in 1946 and *Vision in Motion* was published posthumously later the same year.

Mondrian, Piet (1872-1944) Dutch painter. A leading member of de STIJL, his early works contain SYMBOLIST and EXPRESSIONIST styles until 1911 when he moved to Paris and was influenced by CUBISM. His work gradually became more abstract, and his interest in horizontal and vertical lines became evident in his *Pier and Ocean* series (from 1913). He advanced his theories on Neoplasticism in the de Stijl magazine and developed the strict geometry of his paintings. His best remembered and most typical works are white and primary colour rectangles bounded by solidly rigid black lines, e.g. *Composition in Yellow and Blue* (1929). Mondrian's ordered and harmonious compositional structure was the antithesis of Expressionism. From 1940 he lived in New York, and other notable works include *Broadway Boogie Woogie* (1942-3) and the unfinished *Victory Boogie Woogie*.

Monet, Claude Oscar (1840-1926) French IMPRESSIONIST painter, whose *Impression: Sunrise* (1872) gave its name to the movement. He came from Le Havre, where his teacher, BOUDIN, encouraged him in outdoor painting. From 1862-3 he studied in Paris, where he met RENOIR and SISLEY, and together they began the direct studies of nature and changing light that was to characterize their works. MANET was an early influence on Monet, but

Monet was more interested in experiment with light and colour, e.g. *Women in a Garden* (1867). In London with PISSARRO in 1870-71 he admired the works of TURNER and CONSTABLE and did a series of paintings of the Thames. Returning to France, he lived for a time at Argenteuil before settling at Giverny. From the 1890s, he concentrated on series paintings of places or objects at different seasons or times of day, recording the effects of changing light and shifting colours, e.g. *Haystacks* (1891) and *Rouen Cathedral* (1894). His paintings from later life, as his eyesight failed him, include the *Waterlilies* series (1899-1926). These are large vibrant canvases in which the subject is so secondary to the light effects that the forms are difficult to distinguish and become almost unintentionally abstracted.

monochrome A drawing or painting executed in one colour only. *See also* GRISAILLE.

montage A technique similar to COLLAGE, where the images used are photographic.

Montañés, Juan Martinez (1568-1694) Spanish sculptor. He lived and worked in Seville, where he carved and painted wooden statues of great dignity and grace. He ran a busy workshop and influenced both his own pupils, e.g. VELAZQUEZ and ZURBARÁN. His best-known masterpiece is the *Christ of Clemency* (1603-6), which is intensely moving in its poignant realism.

Moore, Henry (1898-1987) British sculptor. He studied at Leeds School of Art and at the Royal Academy and during the 1930s was involved in the same avant-garde circles as Ben NICHOLSON and Barbara HEPWORTH. He was responsible for reviving the popularity of direct carving methods, disliking the accepted methods of modelling and casting pieces of sculpture. AFRICAN and Mexican art had a profound influence on his works, in which mass and solidity take precedence over suface texture and detail, e.g. *Reclining Figure* (1929). Despite the abstract form of much of his work, the exploration of human relationships is evident in pieces such as *Two Forms* (1934). The latent energy and enormous presence of his sculptures became predominant as essentials were pared away. He explored the idea of pierced and hollowed masses, and the relationships of figures to landscape, e.g. *Reclining Figure* (1938). As a sculptor and draughtsman he was distinguished with awards from the art world and the civic world alike. Other notable works include his drawings from London Underground station shelters when he was a war artist during World War II.

Morisot, Berthe (1841-95) French painter. She was a pupil of COROT and also of MANET, whose brother she married. She was instrumental in encouraging Manet to paint outdoors and to experiment with IMPRESSIONIST colours. She exhibited in all but one of the Impressionist shows and had 13 paintings at the London Impressionist Exhibition of 1905. Typical works include *The Cradle* (1873) and *Jeune Femme au Bal* (1880).

Morris, William (1834-96) English designer, writer, artist and craftsman. Morris was a social reformer who believed that people would be enabled to do better work if they had beautiful surroundings, and to this end he was instrumental in founding the ARTS AND CRAFTS MOVEMENT. He drew his inspiration from the medieval guild systems of the Middle Ages, convinced that utility and art were inseparable. He formed a manufacturing and decorating company producing wallpapers, fabrics and artefacts, and also started the Kelmscott Press to produce a better quality of books in a range of typefaces. The artist BURNE-JONES was one of several who worked for the company, and Morris's own elegant style in some ways anticipated ART NOUVEAU.

Moses, Grandma [Mary Anne Robertson] (1860-1961) American painter. She was entirely self-taught and was discovered by the collector L. J. Calder through a small exhibition of paintings and embroideries in her local drugstore. The simplistic directness of her style and her bright, uncomplicated colours soon won her popularity and success. She had a one-man show at the age of 80 in New York in 1940, and her 100th birthday was declared a state holiday. Her works are a romantic and unsophisticated record of country life in her native New York State.

Motherwell, Robert (1915-) American painter. Originally a graduate in philosophy and an aesthetics theorist, he took up painting professionally in 1941. Influences include PICASSO and MATISSE, although his work is mainly in the ABSTRACT EXPRESSIONIST tradition. He experimented with COLLAGE and with colour staining, developing his compositions with black or white lines. Notable works include the series *Elegies to the Spanish Republic* begun in 1949. He also wrote a great deal on art and artists and produced a series of publications entitled *The Documents of Modern Art* (from 1944).

Mucha, Alfons (1860-1939) Czech painter, designer and graphic artist famous for his ART NOUVEAU posters for the actress Sarah Bernhardt in the 1890s in Paris. In Prague he designed the decor for the burgomaster's room in the municipal hall, windows for the Cathedral and his country's first banknotes and stamps. Part of his *Slav Epic* (1910s-20s) paintings were shown in the US but are now stored in Czechoslovakia.

Munch, Edvard (1860-1944) Norwegian painter. He studied in Oslo and was influenced by IMPRESSIONIST and SYMBOLIST works during visits to France in the 1880s. GAUGUIN'S use of colour was particularly influential in the development of his emotional expressionism. Much of Munch's painting reflects a morbid obsession with sickness and isolation. The imagery is like a recurring nightmare, angst-ridden and violent in its distortion of line and powerful contrasts of blacks and reds. His best-known work, *The Scream* (1893), is typical of his most creative period. After recovering from a nervous breakdown in 1908, Munch's works take on a brighter more optimistic atmosphere. He carried out a series of murals for Oslo University and left most of his works to the city of Oslo, where it is housed in the Munch Museum.

Murillo, Bartolomé Esteban (1618-82) Spanish painter
from Seville whose early works were influenced by his
older contemporary ZURBARÁN. He established his own
reputation with a painting cycle for the Seville
Franciscan Monastery in 1645-46 and became the first
director of the academy in Seville in 1660. He painted
religious and genre scenes popular for their pretty senti-
mentality; soft draperies and misty backgrounds gave an
appealing quality to his work. His reputation was high
during the 18th century but declined thereafter. Large se-
lections of his work are in the Prado, Madrid, and the
Museo de Belles Artes, Seville.

N

Nabis A group of painters working in France in the 1890s. Principal members of the group were SÉRUSIER and VUILLARD. Influenced by the works and ideas of GAUGUIN and by oriental art, they worked in flat areas of strong colour, avoiding direct representation in favour of a symbolic approach of mystical revelation.

Naive Art Works by untrained artists whose style is noted for its innocence and simplicity. Scenes are often depicted literally, with little attention to formal perspective and with an intuitive rather than studied use of pictorial space, composition and colour. Naive painters have existed in various countries throughout the 20th century, independently of contemporary trends or movements in art, and their works are often fresh and invigorating by comparison. Notable naive painters include "Douanier" ROUSSEAU and Grandma MOSES.

Nanni di Banco (*d*.1421) Florentine sculptor. He was taught by his father, and the bulk of his work was commissioned for Florence Cathedral and the Or San Michele. He was greatly influenced by the ANTIQUE and by his contemporary DONATELLO, although the large number of his undated works makes the extent of his own innovations difficult to trace. Early works, e.g. *St Luke* (1408-13), show a graceful, elongated fullness of form that suggests the influence of Gothic art, while his mature masterpiece, *The Assumption*, combines the natural force and vigour of a Donatello sculpture with ideal Antique proportions.

Nash, Paul (1889-1946) English painter and illustrator. He was an official war artist in both World Wars and founded the avant-garde group Unit One in 1933. Essentially a landscape artist, his works are enhanced by an empathy with the land that helps to express the horror and devastation he witnessed in war, e.g. *We are making a new World* (1918). The influences of SURREALIST art and the works of de CHIRICO are evident in works such as *Monster Field* (1939). A major painting from World War II is *Totes Meer* (1940-41). Nash also carried out a number of exceptional book illustrations, in particular the twelve woodcut pictures of the story of creation from the Book of Genesis commissioned by the Nonesuch Press, and the drawings for *Urne Burial* by Sir Thomas Browne.

Nasmyth, Alexander (1758-1840) Scottish painter. He studied in London under Allan RAMSAY, and afterwards in Rome. On his return to Edinburgh he became a portrait painter but he soon abandoned portraits for landscape paintings of great simplicity and beauty.

Navarrete, Juan Fernández (1526-79) Spanish painter from Navarre, who studied in Italy, possibly under

TITIAN, and from 1568 was court painter to Philip II of Spain. Out of the naturalistic Spanish tradition he evolved a unique style reflecting the monumental heroism of his Italian training. His works for Philip II in the Escorial are still in situ, and of the 36 paintings commissioned in 1576 for the Escorial Church, he completed eight before he died. His later works, notably *The Burial of St Lawrence* (1579), anticipate CARAVAGGesque effects of chiaroscuro.

Nazarenes An art movement based on the Brotherhood of St Luke formed in Vienna in 1809. It involved painters of German and Austrian origins, who worked mainly in Italy. Inspired by the medieval guild systems, they worked cooperatively with a common goal of reviving Christian art. Influences included German medieval art and Italian RENAISSANCE painting. Notable among their works are the frescoes of the *Life of St Joseph* (1816-17) for the Casa Bartholdy in Rome, which are now housed in Berlin. A leading member of the group was CORNELIUS.

Neoclassicism A movement in art and architecture in the late 18th and early 19th centuries that followed on from, and was essentially a reaction against, BAROQUE and ROCOCO styles. Classical forms were employed to express the reasoned enlightenment of the age, and Neoclassical painters, such as CANOVA and DAVID adhered to the Classical principles of order, symmetry and calm. At the same time, they felt free to embrace Romantic themes, and much of David's work in particular is charged with emotion in a tensely controlled form. *See also* CLASSI-CISM.

Neo-Impressionism A scientific and logical development of IMPRESSIONISM pioneered by the pointillist painters SEURAT, SIGNAC and PISSARRO. The brokenly applied brushwork of MONET and RENOIR was extended and refined to a system of dots of pure colour, applied according to scientific principles, with the intention of creating an image of greater purity and luminosity than had hitherto been achieved.

Neue Sachlichkeit A German term meaning "New Objectivity," it was originally the title of an exhibition of postwar figurative art planned in 1923 by Gustave Hartlaub, director of the Mannheim Kunsthalle. It then came to represent any art concerned with objective representation of real life; such works were the opposition movement to EXPRESSIONIST subjectivity. Artists associated with the term include BECKMANN, DIX, and GROSZ.

Nevelson, Louise (1899-) Russian-born American sculptor, she trained in Munich and settled in the US from 1905. Typical of her works are her large-scale ASSEM-BLAGES created out of shallow boxes filled with found wooden objects and sprayed with black, white or gold paint, e.g. An *American Tribute to the British People (Gold Wall)* (1959).

Nevinson, Christopher Richard Wynne (1889-1946) English painter. He published the English Futurist mani-

festo, *Vital English Art* (1914), along with the poet
Marinetti. Although a leading figure in British FUTURISM,
his work was also influenced by the Vorticist Wyndham
LEWIS, as in *Returning to the Trenches* (1915). Later
works, such as *Twentieth Century*, are more traditional in
approach.

Newman, Barnett (1905-70) American painter. He
trained at the Art Students' League and was a pioneer of
ABSTRACT EXPRESSIONISM along with ROTHKO and MOTHER-
WELL. Typical of his own style is *Onement* (1948), a
monochromatic COLOUR FIELD painting with a single vertical stripe of lighter colour in the centre. His use of
very large-scale canvases, sometimes irregularly
shaped, greatly influenced other abstract expressionist
painters.

Nicholson, Ben (1894-1982) English artist who studied
briefly at the Slade School of Art but was otherwise
largely self-taught. Early works developed from his own
interpretation of CUBIST principles and were mainly figurative, e.g. *Fireworks* (1929) and *At The Chat Botte*
(1932). From 1933 he began low-relief plaster carvings
in a geometrically abstract style, e.g. *White Relief*
(1935). He was also a member of the avant-garde circle
of artists that included Henry MOORE, Paul NASH and
Barbara HEPWORTH, to whom he was married (1932-51).
After World War II he acquired an international reputation, winning numerous prizes and awards for works that
throughout his versatile career had a stamp of consistent

good taste. Notable later works include *Carnac. Red and Brown* (1966) and *Tuscan Relief* (1967).

Noguchi, Isamu (1904-   ) American sculptor who was brought up in Japan and returned to the US in 1917. He trained with BRANCUSI in Paris, and his early works involve highly polished sheet-metal abstractions. He was also influenced by oriental art in his ceramic and brush drawing works. He won commissions for works as diverse as a *Play Mountain* (1933) for New York City Parks and a Japanese Garden for UNESCO in Paris. While working on the FEDERAL ARTS PROJECT he did a sculptured mural, *History of Mexico* (1935), in Mexico City. Other notable works include *Bridge Sculpture* for Peace Park, Hiroshima. A retrospective exhibition of his work was held at the Whitney Museum of American Art in 1968.

Nolan, Sir Sidney (1917-92) Australian painter. He took up painting at the age of 21 and was almost completely self-taught. Early works are mainly abstract, but he established his reputation with SURREAL figurative works based on themes from Australian history and legend. He worked in a fluid, painterly style, often using unusual surfaces, e.g. glass, which enhanced the liquid translucency of his brushwork. Notable works include the series on Ned Kelly begun in 1946, e.g. *Kelly at Glenrowan* (1955). He also did cover illustrations for the books of his friend, the novelist Patrick White.

Nolde, Emil (1867-1956) German painter. Born Emil

Hansen, he changed his name to that of his home town in 1904. Originally trained as a woodcarver, he studied painting in Munich and in Paris, settling in Berlin in 1906. He was briefly a member of Die BRÜCKE, but maintained an essentially individual style of EXPRESSIONISM. His works are inspired by deep religious feeling and mysticism, his imagery influenced by tribal art, all expressed through violent distortion and clashing colours. Notable among his works are *Dance around the Golden Calf* (1910) and *Masks and Dahlias* (1919). He was classed as a degenerate by the Nazis, and his later works include "unpainted paintings," small watercolours that he painted in secret.

O

objet trouvé *see* **found object**.

odalisque A term in art for a painting of a reclining female nude figure often wearing the baggy trousers of a Middle Eastern female slave. MATISSE painted a series of odalisques.

oeuvre The French word for "work," used in art to denote the total output of an artist.

oil paint A paint made by mixing colour pigments with oil (generally linseed oil) to produce a slow-drying, malleable sticky substance. Oil paint has been the dominant medium in European art since the 15th century because of the range of effects that can be produced.

O'Keefe, Georgia (1887-1986) American painter. Her early works are inspired by the Texan landscape, but most of her art concerns precisionist abstraction of observed forms, often using the technique of isolating one detail in close-up. Her work was exhibited from 1918 at the 291 Gallery owned by the American photographer **Alfred Stieglitz** (1864-1946), whom she married in 1924. Later abstractions suggest empty landscapes and city scenes, or organic forms, e.g. *Black Iris* (1926).

Oldenburg, Claes (1929-) Swedish-born American

sculptor, one of the originators of pop art. He won popular acclaim with *Dual Hamburger* (1962), which formed part of a display of giant foodstuffs and other objects on sale at his shop, "The Store," in New York. He challenged the accepted nature of things with wit and humour, creating "soft" hardware objects and playing with scale and texture.

Olitzki, Jules (1922-) Russian-born American painter who studied in New York and Paris. His early works are in a thick impasto style, but from 1960 he began to experiment with colour staining and with spray-gun techniques. Throughout his work there is a common thread of interest in the edges of the canvas, where most of the pictorial imagery and gestural significance of his work occurs. A typical work is *Pink Alert* (1966).

op art *or* **optical art** An ABSTRACT ART that uses precise, hard-edged patterns in strong colours that dazzle the viewer and make the image appear to move. The principal artists in this field are VASARÉLY and the British painter **Bridget Riley** (1931-), who for a while worked solely in black and white.

Orcagna [Andrea di Cione] (*fl.*1343-68) Florentine painter, sculptor and architect. His masterpiece and only certain dated work is the altarpiece, *The Redeemer with the Madonna and Saints* (1354-57), in the Church of Santa Maria Novella. Its vivid colours and shallow picture plane reflect a more Byzantine style than the naturalism of GIOTTO, although the figures are solidly modelled in a Gothic vein. His sculptures adorn the Tabernacle in the Or San Michele, and other important works attributed to him include the remains of *The Triumph of Death*, *Last Judgement* and *Hell* frescos in Santa Croce. His brothers, **Nardo** (*fl.* 1346-65) and **Jacopo** (*fl.* 1365-98) also worked in the family studio.

Orley, Bernard van (*c.*1488-1541) Netherlandish painter and designer, known as "RAPHAEL of the Netherlands" because of the influence of the art of Raphael on his work. He was also influenced to an extent by DÜRER, whom he met in 1520. He painted portraits at the court of the Regent, Margaret of Austria, where he was official court painter. Notable works include *The Ordeal and Patience of Job* (1521). He also designed tapestries and stained glass.

Orozco, José Clemente (1883-1949) Mexican painter. He trained in architectural drawing but after the loss of his left hand and eye in an accident he taught himself painting. He worked as a cartoonist for various publications, including *La Vanguardia*. He admired the work of MICHELANGELO, and his early paintings are also influenced by POST-IMPRESSIONISM. He was comissioned to paint a large number of murals and frescos, of which *An Epic of American Civilization* (1932-4) is a notable example. His mature work reveals an interest in the geometric abstractions of LÉGER, and his last masterpiece is the emotive and powerful *Hidalgo and Castillo* (1949).

Orpen, Sir William (1878-1931) Irish-born English

painter, a friend and contemporary of Augustus JOHN. He established himself as a successful society portraitist in the fashion of SARGENT, although his own costume self-portraits and his group portraits are generally works of better quality and insight. Some of his most outstanding work was done as an official war artist in World War I, e.g. *The Signing of the Peace Treaty at Versailles* (1919-20) and *Dead Germans in a Trench*.

Orphism *or* **Orphic Cubism** A brief but influential art movement developed out of CUBIST principles by the artists DELAUNAY, LÉGER, PICABIA, DUCHAMP and KUPKA. Their aim was to move away from the objectivity of Cubism towards a more lyrical and colourful art. The artists were influenced in part by Italian FUTURISM, and typical works use juxtaposed forms and strong colours. The term Orphism was coined by the French poet Guillaume Apollinaire in 1912, and the movement had a deep influence on the German Expressionists MACKE and MARC, and on SYNCHROMISM.

Ouwater, Albert van *see* **Bouts, Dieric**.

P

Pacheco, Francisco (1564-1654) Spanish painter, poet and writer from Seville, who was the teacher of VELAZQUEZ, who later became his son-in-law. His most important contribution to Spanish art history is his book, *The Art of Painting* (1649), and his finest work is *The Immaculate Conception* (c.1621).

Pacher, Michael (*fl.c.*1645-98) Austrian painter and sculptor. He worked in an advanced style of the Late Gothic tradition, given the full modelling and lively gesture of his figures within the carved tracery confines of their Gothic architecture settings. A sound knowledge of the works of MANTEGNA is evident in his sensitive use of space. His masterpiece is the *Wolfgang Altarpiece* (1481), and another notable work is *The Four Doctors of the Church* (c.1483).

Palmer, Samuel (1805-81) English painter and engraver. He painted pastoral landscapes, and *A Hilly Scene* (c.1826) is typical of his most intensely creative period, which was spent at Shoreham in Kent. He was acquainted with BLAKE, who deeply influenced the visionary mysticism of his work

Paolo, Veneziano (*fl.* 1321-62) Venetian painter who executed a number of important state commissions, including the cover for the Pala d'Oro in the Church of San Marco (1345). His large polyptych altarpieces have a strong Byzantine feel for colour and decoration. His sons **Luca** and **Giovanni** were also painters, the former collaborating with him on the Pala d'Oro.

Paolozzi, Eduardo (1924-) Scottish sculptor and printmaker of Italian parentage. Major influences on his work include DADA and SURREALISM. He questioned the accepted values of art in his *Bunk* series of COLLAGES. Sculptural images of figures and animals were created from found pieces of machinery and cast in bronze, e.g. *St Sebastian No 2* (1957). Later works, such as *The City of the Circle and the Square* (1963-66), embrace some of the lighthearted elements of pop art.

Paret y Alcazar, Luis (1746-99) Spanish painter of versatile talent, he painted historical, mythical and religious scenes as well as landscapes and still lifes. His ROCOCO genre paintings have a lasting charm that recalls the works of FRAGONARD. He was one of the outstanding artists of his time, surpassed only by GOYA. The Prado, Madrid, houses a good selection of his work.

Parmigianino [Girolamo Francesco Maria Mazzola] (1503-40) Italian MANNERIST painter and etcher of precocious talent. His early works were influenced to an extent by CORREGGIO, and he was familiar with the works of RAPHAEL and DÜRER. His religious compositions are subtle, elegant and gracefully elongated, while his portraits are more directly realistic. An early masterpiece is *The Vision of St Jerome* (1526-7), and his best-known mature piece is *The Madonna of the Long Neck* (*c*.1535). His works were widely known through engravings and through his own innovative use of the etching medium. He had a profound influence on French Mannerist painting.

Pasmore, Victor (1908-) English painter. His early landscapes were influenced by WHISTLER, and he was a founding member of the Euston Road School in 1937. During the 1930s he was interested in objective abstraction, and he later experimented with COLLAGE before finding his niche in CONSTRUCTIVISM. The bulk of his mature work is strictly geometric abstraction, although he later incorporated more organic forms. Typical works include *Evening, Hammersmith* (1943) and *Triangular Motif in Pink and Yellow* (1949).

pastel A paint medium of powdered colour mixed with gum arabic to form a hard stick. When app-lied to paper, the colour adheres to the surface. Pastel was used to great effect by CHARDIN and, particularly, DEGAS.

Paton, Sir Joseph Noel (1821-1901) Scottish painter who studied for some time at the Royal Academy in London. He specialized in allegorical, historical and biblical scenes and first attracted attention with his outline etchings illustrating works by Shakespeare and Shelley. He worked in a style similar to that of the PRE-RAPHAELITE BROTHERHOOD. His first picture to be exhibited was *Ruth Gleaning* (1844) and later works include *The Reconciliation of Oberon and Titania*. He was a prolific painter, and engravings of many of his works, e.g. *The Pursuit of Pleasure: Home* (depicting a soldier's return from the Crimean War) and *In Memoriam* (a scene from the relief of Lucknow), became very popular.

Peale, Charles Willson (1741-1827) American painter. He trained in London under WEST, and from 1775 he lived in Philadelphia where he painted portraits in the NEOCLASSICAL tradition. Famous works include *The Exhumation of the Mastodon* (1806) and *Staircase Group* (1795). Of his seventeen children, five became artists, the three most important being **Raphaelle** (1774-1825), who was a gifted still life painter, his best-known work being *After the Bath* (1823); **Rembrandt** (1778-1860), who was a portrait painter like his father; and **Titian Ramsay** (1799-1885), who was a painter of natural history.

pencil A mixture of graphite and clay in stick form and covered by a hard casing. The greater the clay element, the harder is the pencil. Graphite replaced lead as the principal component in the 16th century. Until the end of the 18th century, the word "pencil" also denoted a fine brush.

Peploe, Samuel John (1871-1935) Scottish painter, who was influenced by CUBISM and the works of CÉZANNE. Richness of colour, fairly formal structure and free brushwork are the hallmarks of Peploe's works. He mainly painted still lifes of flowers, although the subject was always secondary to his painterly style. He also painted series of landscapes of the island of Iona.

perspective In art, the representation of a three-dimensional view in a two-dimensional space by establishing a vanishing point in the distance at which parallel lines converge, the objects or figures in the distance being smaller and closer together than objects or figures nearer the viewer. Perspective is demonstrated in the works of GIOTTO, and its rules were formulated by ALBERTI in *De Pictura* (1435), but by the 20th century these were being abandoned by artists.

Perugino, Pietro [Pietro Vannucci] (*c*.1445-1523) Italian painter, possibly a contemporary of LEONARDO in VERROCCHIO's studio in Florence. He took his name from his native Perugia, where he mainly worked. He painted *The Giving of the Keys to St Peter* fresco (*c*.1481) in the Sistine Chapel, Rome, and also produced portraits and altarpieces in the course of his career. A peaceful serenity pervades his work, as in the gentle and graceful *Virgin and Child*. RAPHAEL was influenced by him, and indeed may have been his pupil, and he was also a source of inspiration for the PRE-RAPHAELITES.

Pevsner, Antoine (1886-1962) Russian-born French painter and sculptor and leading CONSTRUCTIVIST artist. He studied at Kiev and St Petersburg and was influenced by CUBISM. Together with his brother NAUM GABO, he worked in Oslo during World War II, returning to teach in Russia in 1917. They published their *Realistic Manifesto* in 1920 but disagreed with the utilitarian approach of TATLIN and RODCHENKO and moved to Berlin in 1922-23. Pevsner settled in Paris from 1924, where he founded the Abstaction-Creation group. Notable works include *Torso* (1924-26) and *Development Column* (1942).

Picabia, Francis (1879-1953) French painter. His early works are in an IMPRESSIONIST style but, influenced by DUCHAMP, he took a more avant-garde direction from 1912 and was involved with the SECTION D'OR group. Notable works include I *see again in memory my dear Udnie* (1914), which shows the influence of Duchamp. He also collaborated with Alfred Stieglitz (*see* O'KEEFE). His works and writings were highly influential.

Picasso, Pablo (1881-1973) Spanish painter, sculptor, designer and illustrator. The son of a drawing teacher, he showed an early precocious talent in works such as *The Girl with Bare Feet* (1895). Of his "Blue" and "Rose" periods in the early 1900s, typical works include *Child holding a Dove* (1903) and *Family of Saltimbanques* (1905). AFRICAN tribal art and the works of CÉZANNE directed the development of his "Negro" period from 1907-9. In 1906-7 he painted *Les Demoiselles d'Avignon,* which was to herald CUBISM and represents a major turning point in modern art. From 1910 to 1916 he worked closely with Georges BRAQUE, developing synthetic and analytic forms of Cubism and experimenting with COLLAGE techniques. A further development is represented by the painting *Guernica* (1937), a tensely emotional expression of the artist's horror at the bombing of the Basque capital by German planes during the Spanish Civil War. While much of his later painting was powerfully expressive, his sculptural pieces, including *Baboon and Young* (1951) are noted for their wit and humour.

Piero della Francesca (*c*.1416-92) Italian early RENAISSANCE painter from Borgo San Sepolcro, who was in Florence in 1439 working on frescoes in San Egidio for DOMENICO VENEZIANO. While there he was deeply influenced by the works of MASACCIO, who inspired the monumental grandeur of his subsequent works, e.g. *The Compassionate Madonna* (1445). From *c*.1460 he was at the court of Federico da Montefeltro of Urbino, and during this time he painted some of his finest masterpieces, including *The History of the True Cross* frescos (*c*.1452-64), *The Resurrection* (*c*.1460) and portraits of Federico da Montefeltro and his wife. Another notable masterpiece is his last major work, *The Madonna and Saints with Federigo da Montefeltro* (*c*.1475). In later years he gave up painting, possibly due to failing eyesight, and concentrated on theoretical works on perspective and mathematics. He had a strong influence on the works of PERUGINO and SIGNORELLI.

Piero di Cosimo (1462-1521) Florentine painter, he trained with Cosimo ROSELLI, from whom he took his name. He was an interesting and unusual character whose development is difficult to establish due to his large number of undated works. He painted mainly scenes featuring mythological creatures and figures and depicting animals in a sympathetic manner. Notable works include *Cephalus and Procris* and *Mythological Subject*. ANDREA DEL SARTO was his pupil.

pietà The Italian word for "pity," used in art to denote a painting or sculpture of the body of the dead Christ being supported by the Virgin, often with other mourning figures.

Pigalle, Jean-Baptiste (1714-85) French sculptor. He studied in Rome and established his reputation with the marble sculpture of Mercury (1744), which is outstanding in its lively naturalism. Notable monumental works include the tomb for Maurice of Saxony (begun 1753). A technically accomplished and naturally versatile artist, he also painted brilliant portraits, including *Self Portrait* (1780) and *Voltaire* (1770-76), and his skill extended to genre scenes of great charm, e.g. *Child with a Birdcage* (1750).

Pilon, Germain (1527-90) French sculptor. His early works are decorative in the MANNERIST style, as in his figures of the Graces for the monument to King Henry II (1560). A much more moving naturalism is expressed in the tomb of the king and his queen, Catherine de' MEDICI, at St Denis (1563-70). Succeeding generations of French sculptors were much influenced by Pilon's early naturalist style, although his later works were more emotionally personal and had less of a following, e.g. *The Virgin of Piety* (*c.*1585).

Piper, John (1903-92) English painter, writer and designer and a leading abstract painter of the 1930s. By the 1940s he had given up abstraction in favour of a more traditionally subjective style. He expounded his theories in *British Romantic Artists* (1942), and was an official war artist from 1940-42, when he recorded outstanding images of the devastation of bombing. He has also designed stained glass for Liverpool Metropolitan and Coventry Cathedrals.

Piranesi, Giovanni Battista (1720-78) Italian artist. Born in Venice, he settled in Rome in 1740 and established his reputation with etchings of architectural views. These are impressive in their scale and grandeur, and his other engraved works, notably the *Carceri d'Invenzione*, also involve an astonishing degree of inventive imagery. He designed the Church of Santa Maria del Priorato in Rome and was extremely influential among NEOCLASSICAL architects.

Pisanello [Antonio Pisano] (*c.*1395-1455/6) Italian painter. He worked in Rome and Venice on frescoes, since destroyed, in collaboration with GENTILE DA FABRIANO who influenced his INTERNATIONAL GOTHIC style. His decorative and detailed works are rich in colour and texture. Excellent draughtsmanship is evident in carefully observed drawings of birds and animals and in the accuracy of his portraits. Notable works include the fresco, *St George and the Princess* (*c*.1435), and the painting, *The Vision of St Eustace*.

Pisano, Giovanni (*fl. c*.1265-1314) Pisan sculptor, one of the leading Italian sculptors of his time. His works are expressive and elegant in the Gothic tradition. Most notable are his high-relief facades for the Cathedral at Siena (1248-96) and the baptistry at Pisa (*c*.1295). Other important works include the statue of the Madonna at the Arena Chapel in Padua. His father **Nicola** (*fl. c*.1258-84) was also a sculptor, famous for the pulpits in the Baptistry at Pisa (1260) and the Cathedral at Siena (1265-68). These are majestic and powerful in innovation and execution, with high-relief figures and architectural forms inspired by classical antiquity.

Pissarro, Camille (1830-1903) West Indian-born French IMPRESSIONIST painter, he moved to Paris in 1855 where he studied with COROT and later met MONET. He was in London from 1870-71 and was influenced by the works of CONSTABLE and TURNER, as in *Lower Norwood, Snow Scene* (1870). He helped organize and exhibited in all eight Impressionist exhibitions, a typical work being *Red Roofs* (1887). During the mid-1880s he experimented with pointillism (*see* NEO-IMPRESSIONISM) but later resumed a freer style of brushwork and employed a less vivid palette. His eldest son, **Lucien** (1863-1744), also experimented with pointillism and was influenced by the English ARTS AND CRAFTS MOVEMENT before establishing his Neo-Impressionist style. Notable among his works is *Rue Ste Victoire, Winter Sunshine* (1890).

plein air The French term for "open air", used of paintings
that have been produced out of doors and not in a studio.
Plein air painting was particularly popular with the BAR-
BIZON SCHOOL and was a central tenet of IMPRESSIONISM.

pointillism *see* **Neo-Impressionism**.

Pollaiuolo, Antonio del (1431-98) Florentine artist who
ran a workshop with his brother **Piero** (1441-96). They
continued the traditions of CASTAGNO and Filippo LIPPI,
both of whom influenced their work. Although they collaborated on many works, including *The Martyrdom of
St Sebastian* (1745), Antonio's superior talent is evident
in his outstanding pen drawings. Their designs for the
tombs of Pope Sixtus IV (1484-95) and Pope Innocent
VIII (1492-98) had a strong influence on the works of
BERNINI, CANOVA and MICHELANGELO.

Pollock, Jackson (1912-56) American painter. A major
figure in ABSTRACT EXPRESSIONIST painting, his early influences include American Indian art. In the late 1930s he
worked on the FEDERAL ARTS PROJECT and explored
mythical and SURREALIST imagery, e.g.*Guardians of the
Secret* (1943). From the 1940s he developed a more abstract and painterly style, creating the works for which
he is best remembered, in which the paint is poured and
splattered over a canvas on the floor, e.g. *Echo, Number
25, 1951* and *Blue Poles* (1953). His style was uniquely
innovative and influential over a whole generation of abstract painters.

polyptych A painting, usually an ALTARPIECE, consisting of two or more paintings within a decorative frame. *See also* DIPTYCH, TRIPTYCH.

Pontormo [Jacopo Carucci] (1494-1557) Italian painter who took his name from his native village in Tuscany. He trained under PIERO DI COSIMO and may have studied with LEONARDO prior to entering the workshop of ANDREA DEL SARTO in 1512. He established his MANNERIST style with *Joseph in Egypt* (*c*.1515) and worked for the MEDICI family from 1520-21. His works are characterized by vivid colours and a graceful dynamism conveying a strong spiritual feeling and sense of grandeur. Influences include MICHELANGELO and DÜRER, and a notable work is *The Deposition* (*c*.1526-28).

pop art A realistic art style that uses techniques and subjects from commercial art, comic strips, posters, etc. The most notable exponents include LICHTENSTEIN, OLDENBURG, and RAUSCHENBERG.

portraiture The art of painting, drawing or sculp-ting the likeness of someone, either the face, the figure to the waist, or the whole person. Portraits vary from the idealized or romantized to the realistic.

poster paint *see* **gouache**.

Post-Impressionism A blanket term used to describe the works of artists in the late 19th century, who rejected IMPRESSIONISM. It was not a movement in itself, and most of the artists it refers to worked in widely divergent and independent styles. They include BRAQUE, PICASSO, CÉ-

ZANNE, GAUGUIN, van GOGH and MATISSE. The name was originated by the English art critic **Roger Fry** (1866-1934), an enthusiastic supporter of modern art, who organized the first London exhibition of Post-Impressionist painters in 1912.

Poussin, Nicolas (1594-1655) French painter. He studied the ANTIQUE in Rome and was influenced by TITIAN and VERONESE, e.g. *The Poet's Inspiration* (c.1628). During the 1630s he developed a more CLASSICAL style and was commissioned to decorate the Grande Salle of the Louvre, but his preference was for easel paintings rather than large-scale decorative works. He was a painstaking worker, completing paintings from numerous drawings and from specially created miniature sets with wax figures. *The Holy Family on the Steps* (1648) marks his achievement of a pure, harmonious classical order. Through his works in figure composition and landscape, he exerted a huge influence and set the standard in painting for almost the next two centuries.

Pre-Raphaelite Brotherhood A movement founded in 1848 by Holman HUNT, MILLAIS and ROSSETTI, who wanted to raise standards in British art. They drew their imagery from medieval legends and literature in an attempt to provide an escape from industrial materialism. They sought to recreate the innocence of Italian painting before RAPHAEL, and were influenced by the works of the NAZARENES. They had a large following, partly due to the support of the critic John RUSKIN, which included BURNE-

JONES and William MORRIS. The movement broke up in 1853.

primary colours The colours red, blue and yellow, which in painting cannot be produced by mixing other colours. Primary colours are mixed to make orange (red and yellow), purple (red and blue) and green (blue and yellow), which are the secondary colours.

Puvis de Chavannes (1824-98) French painter. He trained under DELACROIX and established his reputation as a decorative mural painter working in oils rather than fresco. His chaste, timeless allegorical works, such as *The Inspiring Muses* (1893-95), were extremely popular and highly influential. *The Poor Fisherman* (1881) is typical of his SYMBOLIST style.

Q

Quarton [Charonton], Enguerrand (*c*.1410-66) French medieval painter. Only two of his authenticated works have survived: *The Virgin of Mercy* (1452) and *The Coronation of the Virgin* (1454). The *Avignon Pietà* has also been attributed to him. His works are characterized by strong light and powerful draughtsmanship, richly illuminated.

Quattrocento An Italian term that refers to 15th century Italian art, often used descriptively of the early RENAISSANCE period.

Queirolo, Francesco (1704-62) Italian sculptor. He worked in Rome and Naples and was influenced by BERNINI. The intricacy of his work is evident in his *Allegory of Deception Unmasked* (1750s) which is of outstandingly high quality.

Quellin, Artus I (1609-68) Flemish sculptor. He studied in Rome and established his reputation as a CLASSICAL sculptor in his decoration of Amsterdam Town Hall (1650-64). He also carried out commissions for portraits and religious sculptures, e.g. *St Peter* (1658). His cousin, **Artus II** (1625-1700), sculpted in a more BAROQUE style, as in *God the Father* (1682), and his nephew, **Artus III**

[Arnold Quellin] (1653-86), who settled in England in 1678, won an important commission for the tomb of Thomas Thynne (1682).

Quercia, Jacopo della [Jacopo di Pietro d'Angelo] (*c.* 1375-1438) Italian sculptor from Siena, a contemporary of GHI-BERTI and DONATELLO. He competed unsuccessfully for the commission for the Baptistry doors of Florence Cathedral in 1401, but went on to create the tomb of Ilaria del Carretto (*c.*1406) in Lucca. This demonstrates an odd mixture of styles, which are more successfully reconciled in a later work, the Fonte Gaia (1409-19) in Siena. His last major commission was for the relief scenes of *Genesis* and *The Birth of Christ* at San Petronio in Bologna, the energetic directness and strength of which were admired by MICHELANGELO.

Quidor, John (1801-81) American painter. He was influenced by Netherlandish painting and by the English satirists HOGARTH and ROWLANDSON. He drew his imagery from literary sources, e.g. *The Return of Rip van Winkle* (1829), but his lively and humorous genre paintings were generally unappreciated, and he was obliged to earn his living as a sign painter.

R

Raeburn, Sir Henry (1756-1823) Scottish painter. He was in London from 1784, where he met Joshua REYNOLDS, then visited Italy before settling in Edinburgh in 1787. He established himself as a society portraitist and held a position in Scotland similar to that of Reynolds in England. He worked directly on to the canvas without preliminary studies or sketches, in a bold, original style. This occasionally resulted in a somewhat flashy superficiality, but still retained a freshness that suited the character of his sitters, e.g.*The MacNab* (*c*.1803-13). Another notable work is the delightfully unusual *Reverend Robert Walker skating* (*c*.1784).

Ramsay, Allan (1713-84) Scottish painter. The son of Allan Ramsay the poet, he studied in London, Naples and Rome, settling in London in 1737. His graceful female portraits, e.g. *Rosamund Sargent* (1749), and his tasteful cosmopolitan air established his popularity. Later works, influenced by French pastellists and a second visit to Rome (1754-57), were lighter and more delicate, culminating in the masterpiece, *The Artist's Wife* (*c*.1755). He ranked alongside his contemporary, REYNOLDS, and his work forms a link between that of

HOGARTH and GAINSBOROUGH. His last major works were the coronation portraits of *George III* and *Queen Charlotte* (1761-2). He gave up painting after an accident in 1773.

Raphael [Raffaello Sanzio] (1483-1520) Italian painter from Urbino, a leading figure of the High RENAISSANCE. He is thought to have studied under PERUGINO, and he was deeply influenced by the works of MICHELANGELO and LEONARDO during a visit to Florence *c.*1504. By the age of 25, he had established enough of a reputation to be summoned to Rome by Pope Julius II, where he painted the *School of Athens* fresco (*c.*1509). He spent the rest of his career in Rome, where he enjoyed huge success and was in such great demand that from *c.*1515 much of his work was carried out by assistants, most notably **Giulio Romano** (*c.*1492-1546), who went on to be one of the major exponents of MANNERISM. Raphael's adaptability and openness to influence, combined with his own self-assurance, helped him achieve the harmony and balance that was to characterize High Renaissance art. His fully human portrayals of the Madonna and the Holy Family are imbued with a deep religious feeling as he combined Christian ideals with the grace and grandeur of classical antiquity. He had a strong influence on TITIAN and was emulated by succeeding generations of painters well into modern times.

Rauschenberg, Robert (1925-) American artist. He trained at Black Mountain College under ALBERS, who influenced his early style. From *c*.1954 he began to experiment with "combine-paintings," in which he applied paint to ordinary objects, e.g. *Bed* (1955). His best-known work in this style is *Monogram* (1959), in which a stuffed goat with a tyre around its middle is splattered with paint after the manner of the abstract expressionists. His works form a link between the introversion of ABSTRACT EXPRESSIONISM and the worldly celebration of pop art. A continuing interest in the relationship between everyday objects and created images is expressed in his screenprints and collages of the 1960s. *Jammers* (1975-6) is typical of his more recent innovative experiments.

Ray, Man (1890-1976) American artist. He studied in New York and founded the DADA group there, along with DUCHAMP and PICABIA. He experimented with SURREALISM and photography, developing the "rayograph," a photographic image created by placing objects directly on to a light-sensitive plate. From 1921-40 he worked in Paris and did some film-making, e.g. *L'Etoile de Mer* (1928).

realism (1) In general, the objective representation of scenes in art. The term is used particularly of the 19th-century French painters, e.g. DAUMIER and COURBET, who broke away from CLASSICISM and ROMANTICISM. (2) Another name for SOCIAL REALISM, the official art in the Soviet Union.

Redon, Odilon (1840-1916) French painter and lithographer. He influenced the SURREALIST movement with his dreamlike images drawn from the works of Edgar Allan Poe and Baudelaire. His pastel drawings of flowers and his portraits make use of intense, translucent colour, e.g. *Silence.* His writings were published in letters and diaries during the 1920s.

Redpath, Anne (1895-1965) Scottish painter, who studied in Edinburgh and worked in France from 1919-1934. Scenes from the Mediterranean coast, villages and church interiors are vigorously painted in thick impasto and rich joyful colour. The still life *Pinks* (1947) is a representative work.

Reinhardt, Ad[olf] (1913-67) American painter, He studied in New York and was a member of the American Abstract Artists from 1947. He experimented with ABSTRACT EXPRESSIONISM and studied oriental art during the 1940s. In the 50s, however, he assumed a more formal style of hard-edged abstraction, and eventually achieved an almost minimalist approach in his *Black Paintings* (1960-62) in which a square canvas is divided into nine equal, barely distinguishable black squares.

relief A sculptural form that is not free-standing. The three-dimensional shape is either carved, e.g. in stone, wood, ivory, etc, or built up, as in metal, etc. Relief sculpture can be *low relief* (*basso relievo* or *bas-relief*), where the depth of the pattern is less than half; *medium relief* (*mezzo relievo*), where the depth is roughly half; or *high relief* (*alto relievo*), where practically all the medium has been removed. The extremely low-relief tech-

nique of *stiacciato*, "drawing in marble," was devised by
DONATELLO.

Rembrandt [Harmensz van Rijn] (1606-69) Dutch
painter, draughtsman and etcher from Leyden. He
trained in Amsterdam where he developed a style akin to
that of CARAVAGGIO, as in *The Stoning of St Stephen*
(1625). He established his reputation as a portraitist with
The Anatomy Lesson of Dr Tulp (1632) and was subsequently in great demand, painting more than 40 commissions in the next two years. In 1634 he married Saskia
van Uylenburgh, and painted the confident *Self Portrait
with Saskia*. He reached the peak of his BAROQUE style in
1636 with *The Blinding of Samson*, and later works are
less dramatic, although more spiritually and psychologi-
cally perceptive, e.g. *Supper at Emmaus*. His series of
self portraits painted over a period of about 40 years reveals the growing insight and depth paralleled in other
works. Youthful exuberance and flamboyant style gives
way to patience, compassion and essential simplicity.
The drama of early works is replaced by a profound,
compelling intensity. As a result, he was less favoured as
a society portraitist, and his genius went unappreciated
except by a few perceptive clients, e.g. *Jan Six* (1654).
Rembrandt died alone and in poverty, having outlived
his wife, his son Titus, and his mistress Hendrikje
Stoffels. He was not mourned nationally, and it was to be
another fifty years before his unique genius and indubi-
table influence were recognized.

Renaissance A term meaning "rebirth." It refers to developments in art, philosophy and culture during the 14th, 15th and 16th centuries. In Italy the early Renaissance in art was established with the works of GIOTTO, in a spectacular move away from Gothic conventions and ideals. The sculptors PISANO and DONATELLO emulated Greek and Roman sculpture in an expression of the new humanist and aesthetic values of the "age of reason." The movement reached a peak between 1500 and 1520 with the works of LEONARDO da Vinci, MICHELANGELO and RAPHAEL. The Northern Renaissance took place as ideas spread to Germany, the Netherlands and the rest of Europe during the early 16th century.

Reni, Guido (1575-1642) Italian painter and engraver from Bologna. After training at the CARRACCI Academy he made several visits to Rome, where he established himself as a leading BAROQUE artist and a rival of CARAVAGGIO with the ceiling fresco *Aurora* (1613-14). He ran a highly productive studio in Bologna, producing mainly religious paintings that maintained their popularity throughout the 17th and 18th centuries. He was an important and influential figure whose works were much imitated.

Renoir, Pierre Auguste (1841-1919) French IMPRESSIONIST painter. He trained in Paris, where he met MONET and SISLEY and began to paint out of doors. He exhibited in the first three Impressionist exhibitions and thereafter pursued his own version of Impressionism, giving more value to perspective, solidity of form and preliminary sketches, e.g. *The Bathers* (*c*.1884-7). Other notable works include *Mme Carpentier and her Children* (1876) and *Moulin de la Galette* (1876).

representational art *see* **figurative art**.

reredos *see* **altarpiece**.

Reynolds, Sir Joshua (1723-92) English painter and art theorist. He trained in London and worked as a portrait-ist in his native Devon. He visited Italy in 1950-52 and developed his theories on the Grand Manner from his studies of RENAISSANCE and BAROQUE painting and CLAS-SICAL sculpture. On his return to London he began to or-ganize his sitters in the poses of classical sculpture, e.g. *Commodore Keppel* (1753). As first president of the Royal Academy, he set high standards in portraiture and history painting, and as a versatile and prolific painter, he enhanced the reputation of English art.

retable *see* **altarpiece**.

Ribera, Jusepe *or* **José de** (called **"Lo Spagnoletto"**) (1591-1652) Spanish painter, engraver and draughts-man. He spent nearly all his career in Italy, where he was influenced by the works of CARAVAGGIO. Notable works include *The Martyrdom of St Bartholomew* (*c*.1630) and *The Clubfooted Boy* (1642). Later works are painted with a lighter palette, and their broadly painted, rich col-ours convey a deepening sense of spirituality, e.g. *The Mystic Marriage of St Catherine* (1648). He was a major influence on Spanish and Italian painting.

Riopelle, Jean Paul (1923-) Canadian abstract painter and sculptor. He founded Les Automatistes along with Borduas in Canada, but settled in Paris from 1946. Early works are lyrical in style, but he gradually developed an interest in surface texture, possibly influenced by Pollock, e.g. *Knight Watch* (1953). His interest in texture is also represented in his sculptural works.

Rivera, Diego (1886-1957) Mexican painter. He studied in Mexico and Madrid and worked in Paris from 1911. His early influences include Cubism, but on returning to Mexico in 1922 he developed a style derived from Mexican and Aztec art. A leading muralist, he carried out commissions for public buildings in Mexico, and later in San Francisco and New York. Notable works include mosaics for the Mexico City National Stadium.

Rivers, Larry (1923-) American artist. He originally trained as a musician and began painting in 1945. Influences include ABSTRACT EXPRESSIONISM and IMPRESSIONISM, from which he developed a painterly, figurative style. He was associated with the younger generation of the New York School. Notable works include *Washington crossing the Delaware* (1953).

Rocky Mountain School *see* **Bierstadt, Albert**.

Rococo A style in art following on from Baroque and even more exaggerated in terms of embellishments and mannered flourishes. It became established around the beginning of the 18th cen-tury and spread throughout Europe, lasting up until the advent of Neoclassicism in the 1760s. The main exponents of the style were FRAGONARD, WATTEAU, and BOUCHER in France and, to a lesser extent, TIEPOLO in Italy and HOGARTH in England. It continued in some areas to the end of the century, particularly in church decoration.

Rodchenko, Alexander Mikhailovich (1891-1956) Russian artist. His early works were influenced by MALEVICH, but he soon developed a more rigorous approach of "non-objectivism". A typical work of this period is *Black on Black* (1918). He subsequently worked in a CONSTRUCTIVIST style, concentrating on line and also producing some delicate hanging sculptures in a similar vein. From 1922 he followed the utilitarian approach of TATLIN, experimenting with photomontage and designing textiles and posters.

Rodin, Auguste (1840-1917) French sculptor. He suffered considerable setbacks in his early career, including three rejections from the Ecole des Beaux Arts. He came to prominence in a whirlwind of controversy over *The Age of Bronze* (1875-6), a male nude figure that he was accused of having cast from life. The vitality of the piece was in fact inspired by the works of DONATELLO and MICHELANGELO, which Rodin had studied during a visit to Italy in 1875. It was bought by the state, who commissioned *The Gates of Hell,* a bronze door for a planned museum of art. It was never completed, although the project occupied most of the rest of his career. Figures for the door, enlarged into independent pieces, include some of his most famous works, *The Thinker*, *The Kiss* and *Adam and Eve*. The rough realism of Rodin's modelling and its intense ROMANTICISM were too radical for the commissioners of the monument to Balzac in 1897, but from 1900 on he won increasing recognition. He was responsible for reviving sculpture as an independent art form rather than as an embellishment or decoration for buildings and monuments. His influence was huge, particularly with the sculptors BOURDELLE and MAILLOL.

Romanticism An art movement dating from the late 18th until the mid-19th century. It was a reaction to the balanced harmony and order of CLASSICISM, and identified with the Romantic writers of the age: Byron, Wordsworth, Goethe, Rousseau and Ossian. In response to increasing industrialization, Romantic painters viewed nature from a nostalgic point of view, imbuing landscapes with powerful emotions, often in a melancholic or melodramatic way. Notable Romantic artists include FUSELI, GOYA, DELACROIX, GÉRICAULT, FRIEDRICH, RUNGE, CONSTABLE, TURNER and the visionary BLAKE.

Rosselli, Cosimo 1439-1507) Florentine painter. He worked on a fresco series for the Sistine Chapel in the Vatican. His own work was pedantic and uninspired but he had the gift of teaching others and ran an important workshop. His pupils included PIERO DI COSIMO and Fra BARTOLOMMEO.

Rosetti, Dante Gabriel (1828-82) English painter and poet. He studied at the Royal Academy, and was a found-

ing member of the PRE-RAPHAELITE BROTHERHOOD. He
worked with BURNE-JONES and William MORRIS on murals for Oxford University Union. His paintings draw on
medieval literature and legend for inspiration. His favourite models included his wife, Elizabeth Siddal, e.g.
in *Beata Beatrix* (1864) and Jane Morris, the wife of
William Morris. His works had an influence on SYMBOL-
ISM.

Rothko, Mark (1903-70) Latvian-born American painter,
a leading figure of the New York School and a pioneer of
COLOUR FIELD PAINTING. Early influences included SURRE-
ALISM, but from the 1950s he worked in an individual
style of ABSTRACT EXPRESSIONISM, creating huge canvases
overlaid with soft rectangular areas of colour, e.g. *Black
on Maroon* and *Red on Maroon* (1958-9).

Rouault, Georges (1871-1958) French painter. He trained
first as a stained glass designer before studying painting
along with MATISSE. He joined the FAUVES in 1904, and
while he made the same use of bright colours, his style
was more influenced by his early training, many of his
paintings resembling stained glass windows. His subject
matter was concerned with human frailty, depicted in images of judges, prostitutes and sad clowns e.g. *Little Olympia* (1906). *Christ Mocked* (*c*.1932) is typical of his religious painting.

Rousseau, Henri Julien ("Le Douanier") (1844-1910)
French painter. He worked in the Paris Toll Office,
which earned him his soubriquet, and took up painting

when he retired in 1885. He exhibited at the Salon des Independants (1886-89, 1901-10) and came into contact with PISSARRO, GAUGUIN and PICASSO in the course of his career. His NAIVE style was unaffected, however, and he continued to defy conventions of colour and perspective in his exotic imaginary landscapes and painted dreams, e.g. *The Dream* (1910).

Rousseau, [Pierre Etienne] Théodore (1812-67) French landscape painter. He painted directly from nature and gained early success with *Forest of Compiegne* (1834), which was bought by the Duc d'Orleans. Over the next decade, however, he was consistently rejected by the Salon, and he became known as *"Le Grand Refusé."* He later became leader of the BARBIZON SCHOOL and exhibited again from 1849. Rousseau's work varied in quality and was always controversial.

Rowlandson, Thomas (1756-1827) English caricaturist and printmaker. He studied at the Royal Academy Schools and in Paris, returning to London in 1777. He worked as a portraitist for a time, then began his famous watercolour caricatures and book illustrations. His popular series of engravings included *The Comforts of Bath* (1798) and *The Tour of Dr Syntax in search of the Picturesque* (1812, 1820 and 1821).

Rubens, Sir Peter Paul (1577-1640) Flemish painter and diplomat. He went to Italy in 1600, studying the works of TITIAN and VERONESE in Venice before entering the service of the Duke of Mantua. During a diplomatic visit to Madrid he painted numerous court portraits and historical scenes. On his return, he began copying famous works of Italian art for the Duke, and his own paintings of this period reflect the influence of the Italian RENAISSANCE. He returned to Antwerp in 1609, and became court painter to the Spanish viceroys, Albert and Isabella. He was already famous when he painted his masterpiece, the triptych *Descent from the Cross* (1611-14). In the 1620s he painted scenes from her life for Marie de' MEDICI in France. In 1628 he was again in Madrid, where he met VELAZQUEZ and painted five portraits of Philip IV of Spain. In 1629 he was envoyed to Britain to negotiate peace with Charles I, and while there he painted *Peace and War*. His last work was *The Crucifixion of St Peter*, and he died in Antwerp. A humanist, he was a man of erudition and culture, and his immense energy and exuberance is reflected in the quality of his work.

Ruisdael, Jacob van (*c*.1628-82) Dutch landscape painter. He joined the Haarlem painters' guild in 1648 and moved to Amsterdam *c*. 1655. His atmospheric landscapes and seascapes are among the most outstanding of the time, anticipating the intuitive perceptions of CONSTABLE. He was never held in great regard by his contemporaries, but gained appreciation in modern times.

Runge, Philipp Otto (1777-1810) German Romantic painter. He studied in Copenhagen and then moved back to Germany, where he met FRIEDRICH and Goethe. His

linear style and allegorical subjects were influenced by
BLAKE and FLAXMAN, e.g. *The Four Phases of Day*
(1808-09).

Ruskin, John (1819-1900) English writer, artist and influential art critic. He came to prominence with his book
Modern Painters (1843) in which he championed the
works of TURNER. This and subsequent writings eventually totalled 39 volumes through which he virtually dic-
tated Victorian taste in art for over half a century. He
supported the PRE-RAPHAELITE BROTHERHOOD, of which
he was a member, being himself a prolific and talented
artist. His personal life was not happy. He was educated
by tutors before entering Oxford University; his marriage was annulled, and his wife married his friend
MILLAIS. During the 1870s he began to lose his reason,
and he lost a notorious libel case against WHISTLER in
1878. His writings and philosophies had a profound influence on the ARTS AND CRAFTS MOVEMENT.

Russell, Morgan (1886-1953) American painter, who
also studied sculpture with MATISSE. In 1913 he co-
founded with MACDONALD-WRIGHT the abstract
SYNCHROMISM movement, although he did not completely renounce more representational works.

Ruysdael, Salomon (1600-70) Dutch landscape painter
and the uncle, and possibly the teacher of, Jacob van
RUISDAEL. His early influences include Elias van de
VELDE, and his works of the 1630s are lyrical in style, but
he gradually developed a fresher palette, e.g. *River*

Scene (1644). His son, **Jacob Salomonsz van Ruysdael** (*c.*1629-1681) was also a painter.

Ryder, Albert Pinkham (1847-1917) American painter. He was reclusive and largely self-taught, and his works have an intense, mystical quality. He was influenced by the Romantic writers, Poe in particular, and painted haunting, macabre pieces, e.g. *The Race Track,* in a bold impasto style.

S

Sacchi, Andrea (1599-1661) Italian painter who was influenced by RAPHAEL, and worked in a strong CLASSICAL style. The ceiling fresco *Divine Wisdom* (1629-33), while not his best work, illustrates his preference for simplicity of composition, involving few figures. His masterpiece is the *Vision of St Romuald* (c.1631).

sacra conversazione The Italian term for "holy conversation", in art denoting a painting in one panel of the Virgin and Child with saints.

Saint-Gaudens, Augustus (1848-1907) American sculptor of French extraction, born in Ireland. He studied in Paris and Rome, where he was influenced by RENAISSANCE sculpture. On his return to the US he established himself as a leading sculptor with the monument to Admiral Farragut (1878-81). His finest work is the Adams Memorial (1891).

salon The French word for "room," which also now denotes an art exhibition (from the Salon d'Apollon in the Louvre in Paris). In the 19th century, the Salon was the annual exhibition of the Académie Française, whose powerful and conventional jury increasingly refused to show the work of innovative artists. In 1863 Napoleon

III ordered that there be an exhibition of artists' work rejected by the Salon, the *Salon des Refusés*. In 1881 administration of the Salon was taken over by the Société des Artistes Français.

Sargent, John Singer (1856-1925) American painter born in Florence. He trained in Paris and caused outrage with the portrait of *Mme X* (1884), which was considered too openly erotic. He settled in London in 1885, where he established himself as a society portrait painter. He was a flattering painter of virtuoso technique and enjoyed immense popularity throughout his career. He also painted outstanding watercolour landscapes and murals.

Sassetta [Stefano di Giovanni] (*c.*1392-1450) Italian painter. He trained in his native Siena, but quickly absorbed the influences of INTERNATIONAL GOTHIC and early RENAISSANCE styles, as in *Madonna of the Snow* (1432). His masterpiece is the *St Francis in Ecstacy* from the St Francis altarpiece (1437-44) created for the Borgo Sansepolcro.

Schiele, Egon (1890-1918) Austrian painter and draughtsman. He met KLIMT while studying in Vienna, and was influenced by ART NOUVEAU, from which he developed his own linear style of EXPRESSIONISM. He caused a scandal with his erotically posed nudes, for which he was arrested in 1912, and some of his works were destroyed. His paintings reveal the influence of Klimt's abstractions e.g. *The Artist's Mother sleeping* (1911).

Schongauer, Martin (*c*.1450-91) German painter and engraver from Colmar. His finest extant work is the *Madonna of the Rose Garden* altarpiece (1437), which indicates the influence of Flemish art, and he was probably familiar with the works of Rogier van der WEYDEN. In engraving he created new standards in subtlety of modelling and delicacy of line, which, combined with a rich imagination, provided a source of inspiration for engravers throughout Europe, including the young DÜRER. A typical example is *The Temptation of St Anthony* (*c*.1470).

school In art, a group of artists who hold similar principles and work in a similar style. In art history, it also denotes that a painting has been executed by a pupil or assistant.

Schotz, Benno (1889-1938) Estonian-born Scottish sculptor. His bronze portraits and figure compositions were cast from freely executed models in clay and other media and have a strong, tactile surface texture. He is well represented in Glasgow, where he lived from 1912, and elsewhere.

Schwitters, Kurt (1887-1948) German painter, sculptor and poet. He studied in Dresden, and his early works are abstract in style. He initiated the Hanover group of DADAists in 1919. He is mainly remembered for *Mertz*, the invented name for his relief COLLAGES and sculptural constructions created from junk materials. From 1920 he began constructing his *Mertzbau*, or large junk constructions, which completely filled his house in Hanover. It was destroyed during World War II. His final *Mertzbau*, unfinished when he died, was constructed at Ambleside in England and is now in the Hatton Gallery, Newcastle-upon-Tyne. *Mertz* was also taken as the name of a Dadaist magazine launched by Schwitters in the 1920s.

Scott, William Bell (1811-90) Scottish painter and poet who trained as an engraver with his father, **Robert Scott** (1777-1841). William showed paintings at the Royal Scottish Academy from 1834 and at the Royal Academy from 1842. His first volume of poetry was published in 1938. In 1843 he became head of the Government School of Design at Newcastle-upon-Tyne. He was acquainted with ROSSETTI and RUSKIN, and his paintings reveal a PRE-RAPHAELITE influence. Some of his best works are contemporary scenes of the North East, e.g. *Iron and Coal*, which was part of a series (from 1855) of history paintings for Wallington Hall, Northumberland. His brother **David Scott** (1806-49) was also a painter, and they were both proficient illustrators.

Sebastiano del Piombo [Sebastiano Veneziano] (*c.*1485-1547) Italian painter, influenced by BELLINI and GIORGIONE in his early works, of which *Salomé* (1510) is a typical example. He moved to Rome in 1511, where he met RAPHAEL and worked with MICHELANGELO, who helped him design his masterpiece, *The Raising of Lazarus* (1517-19). The rest of his major work was in portraiture, e.g. *Clement VII* (1526). In 1523 he became

Keeper of the Seals to Pope Clement VII, which earned him his nickname "del Piombo."

secondary colours *see* **primary colours**.

Section d'Or A group of painters associated between 1912 and 1914 whose aim was to hold group exhibitions and to encourage debate of their aesthetic ideals. They admired the works of CÉZANNE and were concerned with harmony and proportion of composition. They also drew inspiration from FUTURISM. Painters involved with the group included the DUCHAMP brothers, LÉGER, KUPKA and PICABIA.

Segal, George (1924-) American sculptor. He was initially a painter in the ABSTRACT EXPRESSIONIST tradition, and was influenced by KAPROW to take up sculpture. He is best known for his plaster figures, cast from life and usually unpainted, placed like frozen ghosts in realistic settings, e.g. *Cinema* (1963).

Seghers, Hercules Pietersz (*c.*1589-*c.*1635) Dutch painter and engraver from Haarlem. He trained in Amsterdam and worked in Utrecht and The Hague. He was an innovative landscape painter, imbuing small canvases with a sense of immense scope and drama. His etchings were of an outstanding quality, and he did experimental prints on various fabrics and tinted papers. He was admired by REMBRANDT, who owned several of his works, but fell into neglect towards the end of his life and was only rediscovered by the art world in 1871.

Serusier, Paul (1863-1927) French painter and founding

member of the NABIS group. He was influenced by GAUGUIN in his symbolic use of colour, e.g. *The Talisman* (1888). He entered the Benedictine school of religious painting at Beuron, Germany, in 1897, and published his theories on colour and proportion in his *ABC of Painting* (1921).

Seurat, Georges (1859-91) French painter and leading figure of NEO-IMPRESSIONISM. He studied at the Ecole des Beaux Arts and developed the system of Pointillism, based on the theories of DELACROIX and recent scientific discoveries about colour. The pointillist painting is composed of tiny areas of pure colour, arranged so as to merge together and present an image of great luminosity when viewed from a distance. It depends on scientific precision and meticulous brushwork and represents a radical departure from the free, intuitive brushwork of the Impressionists. Important works include *La Grande Jatte* (1884-6), *The Parade* (1887-88) and *The Circus* (unfinished when he died in 1891). He was also an outstanding draughtsman and had a great influence on contemporary and succeeding generations of painters.

Sezession The German word for "secession," adopted as a name in the 1890s by groups of painters in Austria and Germany when they broke away from official academies to work and exhibit in contemporary styles, e.g. IMPRESSIONISM. In Germany, the first German Sezession was in Munich in 1892, followed by the Berlin Sezession of 1899, led by BECKMANN and LIEBERMANN, which in turn in 1910 repudiated the works of Die Brücke, which resulted in the latter group forming the Neue Sezession. In Austria, the Vienna Sezession was organized by Klimt in 1897.

sfumato *see* **Leonardo da Vinci**.

Sickert, Walter Richard (1860-1942) German-born English painter of Danish extraction. He studied with Whistler and was influenced by him and by Degas, whom he met in 1885. In 1905 he established a studio in London, which became a focal point for young English painters. His subject matter is concerned with the sordid realities of urban life, as in his best-known work, *Ennui* (c.1913).

Signac, Paul (1863-1935) French painter. Along with Seurat he was a pioneer of pointillist techniques, and he exhibited some of his works at the last Impressionist Exhibition in 1886. He published his theories on the scientific application of colour in *From Delacroix to Neo-Impressionism* (1899). He later developed a freer style and brighter palette, which influenced the works of Matisse.

Signorelli, Luca (*fl.*1470-1523) Italian painter, possibly taught by Piero della Francesca, whose influence can be seen in *Madonna and Child* and *Flagellation* (c.1480). The drama of *Mother and Child with Saints* (1484) also shows the influence of the Pollaiuoli. From 1484 he worked on some of the frescoes for the Sistine Chapel and later painted his masterpiece, *The Last Judgement* fresco cycle in Orvieto Cathedral (1499-

1502). He was an outstanding draughtsman, his depictions of the male nude being particularly noteworthy.

Simone Martini (*c.*1285-1344) Italian painter from Siena, who succeeded DUCCIO as the leading figure in Sienese painting. Early works include the *Maestà* fresco (1315), for the Siena Town Hall, and *St Louis* (1317). The graceful, linear style and rich decor of his mature works reveal the influence of French Gothic art, as in *Christ Reproved by His Parents* (1342). Other notable works include the frescoes of *Guidoriccio da Fogliano* (1328) and the *Annunciation* (1333).

Sisley, Alfred (1839-99) French painter of English extraction. Early works reveal an admiration for COROT, but he came under the influence of the Impressionists RENOIR and MONET while studying in Paris. He painted mainly peaceful landscapes, carefully composed and sensitively coloured in a pointillist manner, e.g. *Floods at Marly* (1876).

sketch A preliminary drawing made by an artist to establish points of composition, scale, etc.

Sloan, John (1871-1951) American painter and, along with Robert HENRI, a founding member of The EIGHT. Trained at the Pennsylvania Academy of Fine Arts, he painted in the American Realist tradition, depicting the back-street life of New York in a warm-hearted and unpretentious style, e.g. *Hairdresser's Window* (1907).

Smith, David (1906-65) American sculptor. His early work experience in a car factory facilitated his technique of cutting and welding metal. Early influences include PICASSO, but from around 1940 he developed his own style with a strong emphasis on surface texture. *Australia* (1951) is typical of his open structuring at this period. Mature works are more concerned with volume, notably his stainless steel *Cubi* series (from the late 1950s), and almost all his pieces explore the relationship of sculpture to its setting.

social realism A form of realism, in which an artist's political viewpoint (usually on the left) affects the content of his work. It is not the same as **socialist realism,** the name given to official art in the Soviet Union, which was intended to glorify the achievements of the Communist Party.

Soutine, Chaim (1893-1943) Lithuanian-born French artist who studied at Vilna and at the Ecole des Beaux Arts in Paris. His influences include EXPRESSIONIST works, particularly those of KOKOSHKA. He painted in a vivid impasto style, mainly landscapes and portraits of great psychological depth, e.g. *The Old Actress* (1924). He influenced the painter Francis BACON.

Spencer, Sir Stanley (1891-1959) English painter, who trained at the Slade School of Art in London. He remained uninfluenced by contemporary art trends and developed his own eccentric idiom, based on personal beliefs and expressed in a precise, simplified style. He painted mainly Biblical themes, transposed into a modern context drawn from his native Berkshire, e.g. *Resur-*

rection, Cookham (1923-27). Other notable works include the mural cycle for the Sandham Memorial Chapel, Burghclere (1926-32).

stabile *see* **Calder, Alexander**.

Staël, Nicolas de (1914-55) Russian-born French painter. Born in St Petersburg, he trained at the Academy of Fine Arts in Brussels and settled in France from 1937. BRAQUE influenced his early style, and from the 1940s he used rectangular patches of colour to depict volume and texture in an abstract manner. Later paintings were more representational and quieter in tone. *The Roofs* (1952) is typical of his best work.

Steen, Jan (1626-79) Dutch painter, who studied in Haarlem and The Hague. He painted genre scenes of domestic and social life with good humour and insight, and enjoyed great popularity. He had a prolific output, and his works varied in subject and in quality. A typical piece is *The Egg Dance* (*c*.1675).

Stella, Frank (1936-) American painter. His earliest works are ABSTRACT EXPRESSIONIST, but from 1959 he developed tightly controlled symmetrical patterns of black stripes, as in *Jill* (1963). In later works he experimented with shaped canvases and bright colours, and during the 1970s developed these themes by using supporting structures splattered with paint and glitter, e.g. *Guadalupe Island* (1979).

stiacciato *see* **relief**.

Stieglitz, Alfred *see* **O'Keefe, Georgia**.

Stijl, De A group of Dutch artists, founded to spread the theories of DOESBURG and MONDRIAN on ABSTRACT ART, principally through the *De Stijl* magazine, which was edited by Doesburg and published 1917-28. The group rejected the representational in art, believing that art's object was to convey harmony and order, achieved by the use of straight lines and geometrical shapes in primary colours or black and white. Their ideas had great influence, particularly on the BAUHAUS, on architecture and on commercial art.

still life A genre of painting depicting inanimate objects such as fruit, flowers, etc, begun by Dutch artists seeking secular commissions after the Reformation and the loss of Church patronage. Within the genre, the *vanitas* still life contains objects symbolic of the transcience of life, e.g. skulls, hour-glasses, etc, while others contain religious symbols, such as bread and wine. In the 18th century, CHARDIN gave new life to the form, and in the 19th century CÉZANNE's use of it in his experiments with structure was very influential on the CUBISTS.

Stuart, Gilbert (1775-1828) American painter, who studied with WEST in London and travelled widely in Great Britain and the US before settling there permanently 1792. He was one of the foremost portrait painters of his time, working in a distinctive painterly style, and capturing the character of his sitters with conviction. He is best known for his many portraits of George Washington, categorized into three basic types, one of which, the *"Ath-*

enaeum" (1796), is featured on the US one-dollar banknote.

Stubbs, George (1724-1806) British painter and engraver, best known for his paintings of horses, of which he had an outstanding anatomical knowledge. He published his *Anatomy of the Horse* (1766) with his own engraved illustrations, beautifully and accurately depicted. The book established his reputation as a horse painter, and he won numerous commissions for portraits of horses, often portrayed with their owners. His works are also distinguished by masterly composition and atmospheric rendition of landscape. *Mares and Foals by a River* (1763-68) and *Horses attacked by a Lion* (1770) give an idea of the range and scope of his works.

study A drawing or painting of a detail for use in a larger finished work.

Suprematism Russian art movement based on principles of non-objectivity. It was begun by Casimir MALEVICH in 1913, and evolved on a parallel with CONSTRUCTIVISM. *White on White* by Malevich is typical of the work of the movement. The influence of SUPREMATISM spread through the BAUHAUS to Europe and the US.

Surrealism Avant-garde art movement of the 1920s and 30s in France, inspired by the dream theories of Sigmund Freud and by the literature and poetry of Rimbaud and Baudelaire. It was begun by the writer and critic **André Breton** (1896-1966), who published his *Manifesto of Surrealism* in 1924. Its influences include the works of de CHIRICO. There were two main trends: Automatism, or free association, was explored in the works of MIRÓ, ERNST and MASSON, who sought deliberately to avoid conscious control by using techniques of spontaneity to express the subconscious. The world of dreams was the source of inspiration for the incongruously juxtaposed, often bizarre, but precisely painted imagery of DALI, and MAGRITTE.

Sutherland, Graham (1903-80) English artist, who trained as an engraver and whose early works are influenced by PALMER. He began painting landscapes in the 1930s, using vivid colours to depict effects of light, and highlighting features of a scene, as in *Entrance to a Lane* (1939). He was an official war artist during World War II and afterwards was commissioned for the *Crucifixion* (1946) at St Matthew's Church, Northampton. He went on to produce some outstanding portraits, notably *Somerset Maugham* (1949) and *Winston Churchill* (1954). The latter was never liked by Sir Winston and was later destroyed by Lady Churchill. Another outstanding work is the tapestry *Christ in Glory* (1962).

Symbolism An art movement in France towards the end of the 19th century. It represented a res-ponse to the intrinsically visual work of the IMPRESSIONISTS and fell into two distinct trends: REDON and PUVIS DE CHAVANNES were inspired by the images of Symbolist Literature; GAUGUIN, van GOGH and the NABIS explored the symbolic use of colour and line to express emotion.

Synchromism An art movement originating in the US in 1913 with the works of RUSSELL and MACDONALD-WRIGHT. They were concerned with the balanced arrangement of pure colour, or "colours together", as in Russell's *Synchromy in Orange: to Form* (1914). The movement influenced a number of American painters.

T

Taeuber, Sophie *see* **Arp, Jean**.

Tatlin, Vladimir (1885-1953) Russian painter and designer. He studied in Moscow, and his early CONSTRUCTIVIST sculptures were influenced by the works of PICASSO, e.g *Painting Reliefs* (1913). His commission for a *Monument to the Third International* was, unfortunately, never executed. During the 1920s he began designing utilitarian objects and theatre sets, and these gradually conformed more and more to officially approved trends in socialist realism.

tempera A paint medium made by mixing colour pigments with egg. It was much used until the 15th century and the development of OIL PAINT.

Terborch *or* **Terburg, Gerard** (*c*.1617-81) Dutch painter, who studied with his father and in Haarlem. He travelled to Italy, England and Germany, where he painted a group portrait at the *Peace Congress of Munster* (1648). From 1654 he settled at Deventer, where he passed the rest of his career painting refined and sophisticated genre scenes and society portraits, e.g. *A Young Man* (*c*.1663).

Terbrugghen, Hendrick (1588-1629) Dutch painter. He trained in Utrecht and travelled in Italy, where he was influenced by the works of CARAVAGGIO. Works such as *The Liberation of St Peter* (1629) and *The Flute Player* (1621) influenced the painters FABRITIUS and VERMEER.

Thorvaldsen, Bertel (1770-1844) Danish sculptor. The son of an Icelandic woodcarver, he trained at Copenhagen and settled in Rome from 1796. He drew his inspiration from ANTIQUE sculpture, and his work is austerely classical. He achieved fame with the statue of *Jason with the Golden Fleece* (1802-3) and enjoyed a successful career. He ranks alongside CANOVA and FLAXMAN as an outstanding sculptor of the NEOCLASSICAL period.

Tiepolo, Giambattista (1696-1770) Italian artist, the greatest decorative fresco painter of the ROCOCO period. From 1737 he was doing fresco cycles characterized by a light, ethereal chiaroscuro, presenting a subtly atmospheric celestial vision. His greatest work is the decor for the Archbishop's Palace in Wurtzburg, including the fresco *The Marriage of Frederick Barbarossa and Beatrice of Burgundy* (1751). From 1762 he worked for Charles III of Spain, and there painted some outstanding religious works for the Royal Chapel, some of which remained unfinished at his death. The preparatory sketches are in the Courtnauld Collection, London. His sons **Lorenzo** (1736-*c*.1776) and **Domenico** (1727-1804) were also painters and assistants to their father. Of the two, Domenico was the more talented and achieved success working mainly in his father's style.

Tiffany, Louis Comfort *see* **Art Nouveau**.

Tintoretto, Jacopo [Jacopo Robusti] (1518-94) Venetian painter, the son of a dyer, or *Tintore*, from whom he took his name. He absorbed the lessons of TITIAN in his use of colour and was inspired by the drawing of MICHELANGELO, as in *The Miracle of the Slave* (1548). The synthesis of these great influences resulted in a dynamic, highly imaginative style of painting, which was to evolve into the MANNERIST tradition and pave the way for the BAROQUE. As his mature style developed, he experimented with the effects of lighting and highlighting, and with a heightened sense of space and perspective, e.g. *The Finding of the Body of St Mark.* From 1564 he worked on the decor of the Scuola di San Rocco, painting scenes from the life of Christ, including a striking *Crucifixion.* One of his last and finest paintings is *The Last Supper* (1592-94). Of his seven children, three became painters: **Domenico** (1562-1635), **Marco** (1561-1637) and **Marietta** (*c*.1556-1590), who was known as "La Tintoretta".

Tissot, James [Jaques Joseph] (1836-1902) French painter and engraver. He trained in Paris and was influenced by DEGAS. He moved to London after 1871 and achieved success with his polished scenes of Victorian society, e.g. *The Last Evening* (1893), which reveal the influence of MANET and WHISTLER. He spent the last 20 years of his life visiting Palestine and painted *c*.300 watercolours on the life of Christ.

Titian [Tiziano Vecelli] (*c*.1490-1576) Venetian painter, one of the greatest figures in world art. He studied under Giovanni BELLINI and was influenced by him and by GIORGIONE, to whom he was an assistant. After the death of Giorgione, many of whose works he completed, Titain was unrivalled in Venice for about 60 years. He achieved fame with *The Assumption of the Virgin* (1516-17), equal in power and grandeur to the best of Rome's talents, but surpassing all in its richness of colour. His subsequent commissions for the Duke of Ferrara include the masterpiece *Bacchus and Ariadne* (1523). From 1530 he was patronized (and in 1533 ennobled) by the Holy Roman Emperor Charles V, portrayed on horseback in *Charles V at Mühlberg* (1548). Philip II of Spain succeeded his father as Titian's patron. His commissions for mythical subjects resulted in the development of Titian's *Poesies*, paintings of earthy sensuality and glowing har-mony of colour, e.g. *Bacchanal* and *The Rape of Europa* (1562). A delicate poignancy pervades the works of his last years, from *The Fall of Man* (*c*1570) and *Christ Crowned with Thorns* (*c.*1590) to *Madonna suckling the Child* (1570-76) and culminating in the beautiful, unfinished *Pietà* (1576). In the course of his career, he painted almost every kind of picture and fully explored the potential of oil paint in his free and revolutionary techniques. His influence on succeeding generations of painters is incalculable.

tondo The Italian word for "round", used in art to denote a circular picture or sculpture.

Toulouse-Lautrec, Henri [Marie Raymond] de (1864-1901) French painter and lithographer. The son of a wealthy aristocrat, ill health in childhood and a subsequent accident, in which both legs were broken, stunted his growth. He trained in Paris, where he met van GOGH and was influenced by the works of DEGAS. His subjects were café clientele—prostitutes and cabaret performers in and around Montmartre, where he lived and worked, e.g. *In the Parlour at the Rue des Moulins* (1894). He is best known for his lithographs and posters advertising cafes and entertainers, such as Aristide Brouant and Yvette Guilbert. Much of his flattened linear style was influenced by Japanese prints.

trecento The Italian term for the 14th century.

triptych A painting, usually an ALTARPIECE, consisting of three hinged parts, the outer two folding over the middle section. *See also* DIPTYCH, POLYPTYCH.

Trumbull, John (1756-1843) American painter. He studied under WEST in London and was influenced by him and by COPLEY, as in the famous *Death of General Warren at the Battle of Bunker Hill* (1786). He painted many scenes from the American War of Independence, also landscapes and some notable portraits of George Washington.

Tura, Cosimo (*c*.1431-95) Italian painter, who studied in Padua and established the School of Ferrara in 1452. His highly individual style was characterized by tortured forms and harsh colouring, creating scenes of tense emo-

tion. This powerful atmosphere is enhanced by an enigmatic use of architectural detail. Notable works include
Pietà and *St Jerome.*

Turner, Joseph Mallord William (1775-1851) English
painter. Of precocious talent, he exhibited his first work
at the Royal Academy at the age of 15. He collaborated
on a series of architectural studies in watercolour, and
from 1796 began painting in oils under the influence of
CLAUDE and WILSON. In 1802 he visited Paris, where the
works of TITIAN and POUSSIN at the Louvre inspired his
developing personal style, as in *The Shipwreck* (1805).
He visited Italy in 1819 and thereafter became more interested in gradations of shifting light and atmosphere,
and bolder in his application of brilliant colours, e.g. *The
Bay of Baiae, with Apollo and the Sybil* (1823). He made
a second visit to Italy in 1829, and the works of the next
two decades represent his finest period. Paintings such
as *The Burning of the Houses of Parliament* (1834), *The
Fighting Temeraire* (1839), *The Sun of Venice going to
Sea* (1843) and *Rain, Steam and Speed* (1844) might
have been painted with the very elements they depict,
and they were described at the time by CONSTABLE as
"airy visions painted with tinted steam." Turner's innovations were not approved by the critics, but he had a
supportive patron in Lord Egremont of Petworth, and an
influential champion in John RUSKIN, who defended him
in *Modern Painters* (1843). He became reclusive in old
age, and died in lodgings in Chelsea, London, under the

assumed name of Booth. He left nearly 20,000 watercolours and drawings and 300 oil paintings to the nation.

Twombly, Cy (1929-) American painter. He studied in Boston, New York and The Black Mountain College before settling in Rome in 1957. He established a distinctive gestural technique based on graffiti and children's art, e.g. *Untitled* (1968). His ideas are informed by SURREALIST Automatism, and he owes a certain debt to KLEE and to RAUSCHENBERG.

Tworkov, Jack (1900-82) Polish-born American painter whose early works were influenced by CÉZANNE. In the 1930s he worked on the FEDERAL ARTS PROJECT and met DE KOONING, who was to influence his later ABSTRACT EXPRESSIONIST style. A typical work of the 1950s is *Duo I* (1956).

U

Uccello, Paolo (*c.*1396-1475) Florentine painter, who trained with GHIBERTI and worked on *Mosaics* in Venice (1425-31). His earliest dated work is the fresco of *Sir John Hawkwood* (1436), and his use of a double viewpoint indicates an interest in perspective that was to dominate all his work. In *The Flood* fresco (*c.*1455) he uses a similar device of two vanishing points to powerfully dramatic effect. Uccello combined RENAISSANCE ideas concerning spatial composition with a Gothic sense of decorative detail in his most famous work, *The Battle of San Romano* (1455), which was painted for the MEDICI Palace. This combination of styles is synthesized to a masterly degree in some of his later works, including *The Night Hunt* (*c.* 1465-9), which is also one of the first paintings on canvas to be painted in Italy.

Utrecht School A movement in Dutch art begun by HONTHORST, TERBRUGGHEN and **Dirck van Baburen** (*c.*1595-1624), who were in Rome between 1610 and 1620 and were strongly influenced by CARAVAGGIO, whose style they took back to the Netherlands, thus influencing in turn such northern masters as VERMEER and REMBRANDT.

Utrillo, Maurice (1883-1955) French painter. He was largely self-taught, encouraged to paint by his mother, the painter **Suzanne Valadon** (1867-1938), and by his adoptive father, the writer Miguel Utrillo. He painted the Parisian streets around Montmartre, e.g. *La Place du Tertre* (*c*.1910) in richly subtle colours and thick impasto. A victim of alcoholism and drug addiction, he was frequently convalescent in nursing homes, but despite this his output was prolific and his paintings much sought after. His palette brightened in his later works, but paintings from his "White Period" (1908-14) represent the peak of his popular achievements.

V

van Gogh, Vincent *see* **Gogh, Vincent van**.

Vasarély, Victor (1908-) Hungarian-born French painter. He trained in Budapest under MOHOLY-NAGY, and in
1930 moved to Paris where he began working in graphic
design. During the 30s he produced the black and white
semi-abstract paintings *Zebras* and *Harlequins*. In the
late 40s his works became completely abstract, and he
later became a leading exponent of op art, with works
such as *Timbres II* (1966). He published his ideas in *Yellow Manifesto* (1955).

Vasari, Giorgio (1511-74) Italian painter, writer and architect from Arezzo, famous as the chronicler of the
RENAISSANCE period in Italian art. The first edition of his
*Lives of the Most Eminent Painters, Sculptors and Ar-
chitects* was published in 1550 and revised and enlarged
in 1568. In it he traces the revival of ancient Roman aesthetic values and the development of art from GIOTTO
and PISANO to MICHELANGELO, coining the term
Rinascente, or Renaissance. It remains a source of prime
importance for modern art historians. As a painter he
trained under ANDREA DEL SARTO and worked in Rome on
decorations for the Vatican and the Cancelleria. He emu-

lated Michelangelo in his MANNERIST style, evidenced in the decor for the Palazzo Vecchio in Florence (from 1563). In architecture, his finest work is the Uffizi in Florence (from 1560), which, appropriately, now houses many of Italy's finest art treasures.

Velazquez *or* **Velásquez, Diego Roderiguez de Silva y** (1599-1660), Spanish painter, the greatest master to come out of Spain. He trained in Seville with PACHECO from 1613 and married Pacheco's daughter in 1618, the year he set up his own studio. His earliest paintings were *bodegones*, a type of genre painting peculiar to Spain, consisting largely of domestic scenes, e.g. *An Old Woman Cooking Eggs* (1618). From 1623 he was court painter to Philip IV at Madrid, painting portraits and some historical events. In 1628 RUBENS visited Madrid, and on his advice Velazquez travelled to Italy, where he was deeply influenced by the works of TITIAN and TINTORETTO. A lighter palette and freer brushwork are evident in his subsequent works. It was on a second visit to Italy that he painted his best single portrait, of *Pope Innocent X* (1650). He also painted one of the most remarkable history paintings, the moving *Surrender of Breda* (1634-35). Notable among his court portraits are *Infante Baltasar Carlos on Horseback* (1635-6), several of the Infantas Margarita and Maria Theresa, and the full-length portraits of *Philip IV* (*c*.1632) and the young queen *Anne Maria of Austria* (1552). His most complex and best-known work is *Las Meninas* (1656), a fine example of his realist style. Overall, his works are distinguished by their unflattering truth to nature, combined with an integrity and respect for the individual, resulting in an overwhelmingly direct character analysis

Velde, Henri Clemens van de (1863-1957) Belgian painter, architect and designer. He studied in Paris, and his early works are in a NEO-IMPRESSIONIST style. From 1893 he was interested in architecture and interior design, influenced by the works of Willaim MORRIS and the ARTS AND CRAFTS MOVEMENT. In 1906 he initiated the Deutscher Werkbund along with his pupil, Walter Gropius (*see* BAUHAUS), and became a Director of the Weimar School of Arts and Crafts. He designed furniture and ornaments in the ART NOUVEAU style, and his building designs disseminated the ideas of Charles Rennie Mackintosh.

Vermeer, Jan *or* **Johannes** (1632-75) Dutch painter. The son of a Delft art dealer, he may have studied under FABRITIUS, but little of his work is documented and the chronology of his development is uncertain. One of his accepted early works is *Christ in the House of Mary and Martha* (*c.*1654). He is best remembered for his small-scale intimate interior scenes, carefully composed and lit, usually by daylight through a window, e.g. *Girl Reading*. Portraits and interiors make up the bulk of his oeuvre, but he left two paintings of the town of Delft: *A Street in Delft* and *A View of Delft*. The latter is notable for its tonal verity and quiet intensity. His business, inherited from his father, failed to support his wife and eleven children, whom he left bankrupt when he died. His full significance as a painter was only recognized in the 19th century, although his works were not unpopular in his day.

Veronese, Paolo [Paolo Caliari] (1528-88) Italian painter born in Verona, one of the outstanding decorative painters of his time. He was indebted to the influence of TITIAN, who encouraged him to settle in Venice in 1553. In the same year he won his first major commission for frescoes on the Doge's Palace, and from 1555-58 he worked in San Sebastiano in Venice on scenes from the *Book of Esther*. He decorated the Villa Maser at Treviso *c.* 1561 and was back at the Doge's Palace from 1575-82. A technical virtuoso, he created scenes of grandeur or anecdotal playfulness with equal confidence. Sumptuous fabrics and sensual figures adorn his magnificent architectural settings and landscapes. The secular quality of his religious paintings, e.g. *The Marriage at Cana* (1562-63) and *The Last Supper* (1573), brought down the wrath of the Inquisition, before whose tribunal he was called to defend his works. As a result, *The Last Supper* was renamed *Feast in the House of Levi.* Veronese's work embodies the last representations of Renaissance ideals.

Verrocchio, Andrea del [Andrea di Cione] (1435-88) Florentine sculptor and painter. Possibly a pupil of DONATELLO, he originally trained as a goldsmith. His earliest important commission was for the sculpture *The Doubting of Thomas* (1465), a beautifully detailed piece. It was followed by his refined *David* (*c*.1475), which rivalled the work of Donatello, as did Verrocchio's masterpiece, the equestrian statue *Bartolommeo Colleoni* (1481-90). Few paintings can be attributed to Verrochio with any certainty, although he ran a large and busy workshop. *The Baptism of Christ* (*c*.1472) is one that owes its fame to the contribution of his celebrated pupil, LEONARDO DA VINCI.

Villon, Jacques [Gaston Duchamp] (1875-1963) French painter, brother of Marcel DUCHAMP and Raymond DUCHAMP-VILLON. He studied in Paris and exhibited at the Salon d'Automne from 1904. From 1911 he worked in a CUBIST style, exhibiting alongside LÉGER and others with whom he formed the SECTION D'OR group. He also had works in the ARMORY SHOW of 1913. Later works explore both representational and abstract themes.

Vingt, Les A group of 20 Belgian painters, including ENSOR, who exhibited together in Brussels for ten years from 1884. Their exhibitions also included works by innovative French painters, e.g. SEURAT, GAUGUIN, CÉZANNE and van GOGH.

Vorticism A short-lived English Cubist art movement devised by Wyndham LEWIS, who also edited the two issues of its magazine *Blast* (1914, 1915).

Vlaminck, Maurice de (1876-1958) French FAUVIST painter, who was influenced in his vigorous approach by the works of van GOGH. He worked alongside DERAIN, and they exhibited together with MATISSE at the famous Salon exhibition of 1905. His painting *The Bridge at Chatou* (1906) is a representative work of the period.

Vouet, Simon (1590-1649) French painter. He was in Italy from 1613-27, and his early works are in the style of CARAVAGGIO. He later adopted a BAROQUE style modified by Bolognese CLASSICISM, as in *The Appearance of the Virgin to St Bruno* (c.1626). He returned to France as court painter to Louis XIII in 1627 and achieved great popular success, establishing a large studio where he taught the major painters of the next generation, including LEBRUN.

Vuillard, Edouard (1868-1940) French painter. A contemporary of BONNARD, he was influenced by Gauguin and by Japanese art in his flattened planes and decorative style. *Mother and Sister of the Artist* (c.1893) is typical of his most important work in its sensitive application of colour and lighting. Later works are more naturalistic.

W

Warhol, Andy (*c*.1928-87) American painter, designer and film-maker of Czech parentage, best known as a pioneer of pop art. He studied at the Carnegie Institute of Technology and worked as a commercial artist before setting up his studio, "The Factory," in the 1960s. He exhibited his first stencilled and silkscreened pieces from 1962, e.g. *Green Coca-Cola Bottles* (1962) and the famous *Campbell's Soup* reproduction, the enduring image of Pop Art. He created multiple image screenprints of famous figures, such as *Marilyn Monroe*, *Elvis Presley* and *Mao Tse Tung*. He made several films, experimenting with long, silent shots filmed from a fixed viewpoint e.g. *Sleep* (1963), which lasted six hours. He also managed the rock band, The Velvet Underground.

watercolour A paint medium of colour pigments mixed with water-soluble gum arabic. When moistened with water, a watercolour paint produces a transparent colour that is applied to paper, usually white, the paper showing through the paint.

Watteau, Jean-Antoine (1684-1721) French painter, an outstanding exponent of the ROCOCO, whose early influences included Flemish art. He moved to Paris from

Valenciennes in 1702 and worked at the Opera as a scene painter before entering the studio of the decorative painter Audran in 1707. He achieved success with *Embarkation for Cythera* (1717) and was accepted as a member of the Academy. Influenced by the works of GIORGIONE and RUBENS, he painted his *Fêtes Gallantes*. Idyllic pastoral scenes of great sensuality, they portray aristocratic figures in court dress or masquerade, sensitively drawn and coloured. Their Rococo atmosphere of frivolity is tinged with a wistful sense of transient pleasure, and the artist himself was already suffering from the consumption that caused his premature death. His final work, *Enseigne de Gersaint* (1721), was drawn from nature and more classically composed, suggesting the potential of a new realism in his work. His many admirers and imitators failed to achieve his delicacy of colour and sensitivity of composition.

West, Benjamin (1738-1820) American painter, who studied in Philadelphia and Rome before settling in London in 1763. He was patronized by George III, and his studio was a focal point for American art students in London. In his great innovative work, *The Death of General Wolfe* (1770), he defied traditions in history painting by depicting his characters in contemporary dress. The precedent was soon copied by COPLEY and other American history painters. His early NEOCLASSICAL style gradually gave way to ROMANTIC themes, e.g. *Saul and the Witch of Endor* (1777) and *Death on a Pale Horse*

(1802). He became President of the Royal Academy in 1792.

Weyden, Rogier van der (*c*.1399-1464) Flemish painter. No signed works by him survive, and his career has been established through documentation in other contemporary sources. He is thought to have trained under Robert CAMPIN, and was influenced by him and by van EYCK. A notable early painting is *The Deposition* (*c*.1435), and his finest work is the *Last Judgment* altarpiece (*c*.1450). His outstanding achievement and the distinguishing quality of his work lies in his ability to convey drama and emotion. Later works, e.g. *The Adoration of the Magi* from the Columba altarpiece, are characterized by the sense of peaceful serenity that marks his portrait work.

Whistler, James Abbot McNeill (1843-1903) American painter. He studied in Paris, and his early works are Realist in style. He settled in London from 1859 and was influenced by the PRE-RAPHAELITE movement, and by Japanese art. He became famous as a portraitist, with works such as *Arrangement in Grey and Black*, a portrait of the artist's mother. He explored the idea of colour harmony in his paintings, and often gave his works musical titles, such as *Chelsea: Nocturne in Blue and Green* (*c*.1870) and *Old Battersea Bridge: Nocturne in Blue and Gold*. His Thames paintings transformed the riverside docks and warehouses into images of misty beauty, but his exhibition at the Grosvenor Gallery in 1877 aroused the acid criticism of RUSKIN. The result was a notorious lawsuit that initiated the mental breakdown of Ruskin and bankrupted the victor, Whistler, who was awarded only a penny in damages. He published his collected writings, *The Gentle Art of Making Enemies* in 1890.

Wilkie, Sir David (1785-1841) Scottish painter, who studied in Edinburgh and settled in London from 1805. He achieved popularity with his genre paintings, which were small in scale and depicted rural festivities and domestic scenes with wit and humour. His *Chelsea Pensioners reading the Gazette of the Battle of Waterloo* (1822) was an immediate success when shown at the Royal Academy. Later works, influenced by the Old Masters, were more serious in subject and grander in approach, e.g. *John Knox preaching before the Lords of the Congregation.* He was also a successful portraitist and etcher. In 1840 he travelled to the Middle East to research material for his Biblical paintings, but he died on the return voyage.

Wilson, Richard (1713-82) Welsh painter and founding member of the Royal Academy. His early works are portraits, e.g. *Admiral Thomas Smith* (*c.*1745). After visiting Italy from 1750-57, he took up landscape painting, influenced by the works of CLAUDE LORRAINE. His classically composed paintings are enhanced by a lyrical freedom of style, e.g. *View of Rome from the Villa Madama* (1753). Some of his finest works were achieved when he applied this style to the landscape of his native Wales, e.g. *Snowdon from Llyn Nantil* (*c*.1770).

Wright, Joseph ["Wright of Derby"] (1734-97) English painter. He spent most of his career in his native Derby, apart from travels to London and Italy (1773-75). He did genre paintings, portraits and landscapes, the outstanding features of which are his extraordinary light effects, e.g. *An Experiment on a Bird in an Air Pump* (*c*.1767).

Wyeth, Andrew (1917-) American painter, who was trained by his father, the illustrator **Newell Covers Wyeth** (1882-1944). Andrew's works are austerely realistic, meticulously painted in watercolour or egg tempera from a generally earthy palette. He painted landscapes and interiors devoid of human presence, and his use of an off-centre compositional device creates a nostalgic, haunting atmosphere. This strange quality also informs his portraits, including the famous *Christina's World* (1948).

Z

Zucchi, Antonio *see* **Kaufmann, Angelica**.

Zurbarán, Francisco (1598-1664) Spanish painter, who lived and worked almost entirely in his native Seville. He painted mainly religious works, apart from a few still lifes and *The Labours of Hercules* series, commissioned by Philip IV. His starkly lit figures of monks or saints were painted in an austerely realistic style, and conveyed an atmosphere of spiritual intensity, e.g. *St Francis*. From 1640 he was rivalled by MURILLO, whose popularity soon outshone his completely, and he retired to Madrid in 1658. Much of his work was exported to South America.